why the new deal matters

yale

university

press

new haven

and

london

eric

rauchway

why the

new deal

matters

Yale University Press books may be purchased in quantity for educational, business, or promotional use. For information, please e-mail sales.press@yale.edu (U.S. office) or sales@yaleup.co.uk (U.K. office).

Set in Adobe Garamond type by IDS Infotech Ltd. Printed in the United States of America.

Library of Congress Control Number: 2020945676
ISBN 978-0-300-25200-2 (hardcover : alk. paper)

A catalogue record for this book is available from the British Library.

This paper meets the requirements of ANSI/NISO Z39.48-1992 (Permanence of Paper).

10 9 8 7 6 5 4 3 2 1

also by eric rauchway

For Kathy

contents

introduction

One winter in the United States there were more people out of work than at any time anyone could remember or records could tell. In the evenings, families throughout the country gathered to enjoy such entertainment as they could find—and afford. Few of them had been able to go anywhere, nor did they have much news the others did not already know. Crisis had grown normal. Hard times had lasted so long, and so shrunk their horizons, that many people grew sick of their housemates and the limits of their lives, constrained by this long emergency, and by uncertainty, and by the inexorable dwindling of their resources and the apparently ineffective actions of everyone to do anything to reverse the destructive inactivity that plagued their nation, and others. Their houses smelled of the few meals they knew how to cook and for which they could get ingredients, and also of fear. For an invisible enemy lurked outside, one that had gathered strength in Asia and in Europe, and that now threatened to pour out its unreasoning malice on the United States. You couldn't see it; you didn't know which of your neighbors might harbor it. So you kept to the people you knew best, you did your work if you still had some, and you hoped that in the evening you might find distraction from the news, all of which was bad.

And then, toward the end of that winter, there was something new to hear, because American voters had made a decision about their country. Even as the unending crush of desperation grew ever worse, they decided to dispense with what they knew and try something else. They had grown tired of sleek men assuring them repeatedly that they needed only to have confidence in the fundamentals of American business and all would be well. They had been told they need not turn to the government at Washington, DC, for help, although the government at Washington, DC, was giving money to help those same sleek, reassuring men, even while it was turning guns on other, poorer people who went to the capital city to ask for aid from their representatives. So the American voters decided they wanted a different government at Washington, one that pledged itself to pull the nation together, to do its utmost to solve their problems and to fight the global contagion of fascism that threatened to engulf them. They voted for a New Deal, which they had been promised would mean federal jobs, laws protecting workers, relief for farmers, and all manner of things that the wisdom of bankers and businessmen had thus far mandated they ought not to have because recognizing these rights would fetter American ingenuity.

And so, with that decision made, and a few last weeks of winter to get through before the spring on which so many had placed their hopes, the families huddled in American homes were able to take comfort one weekend, for the first time in a long time, in what the president of the United States had to say to them: that with the "money changers" out of power, it was time to "apply social values more noble than mere monetary profit." The president promised the "joy and moral stimulation of work." The country must pull together, and "realize as we have never realized before our interdependence." None of us alone could survive, or prosper, so well as if we all worked to survive and prosper together. That way, we could ensure "the future of essential democracy."[1]

The New Deal mattered then, at the cusp of spring in 1933, because it gave Americans permission to believe in a common purpose that was not war. Neither before nor since have Americans so rallied around an essentially peaceable form of patriotism. The results of that effort remain with us, in forms both concrete and abstract; the New Deal therefore matters still because Americans can scarcely get through a day without coming into contact with some part of it.

It matters, too, as a message for Americans from the past: democracy in the United States, flawed and compromised as it was, proved it could emerge from a severe crisis not only intact but stronger. Even at that moment, in that winter, the nation of Germany was taking a different path than the one of "essential democracy." When the New Deal began, fascism was on the march around the world and its agents were working within the United States; it ended with the United States and its allies triumphant over that ideology and establishing a New Deal for the world—or at least a framework for one—and an improved democracy within the United States.

We might do well to heed that message now, taking note of our predecessors' successes and failures alike as we consider how we can find our way out of a hard, strange, isolated winter of our own.

When I started writing this book, I wanted to show how easy it was to point out how much the New Deal matters to our daily lives. You don't even really need to know where to look; you just need someone to tell you what you're looking at: evidence of the New Deal is everywhere even now, nearly a hundred years since it started. I walked for ten minutes, over to the library on the campus of the University of California, Davis, where I work, and sat in the reading room there. Readers and writers always crowd the desks; it is a fine spot for us on account of its high ceilings and the good light that fills the space. I wanted to count the windows myself so I could report them to you: there are nine, each nearly two hundred feet square. There are also twenty-seven custom-designed, streamlined, aluminum chandeliers with frosted glass. Under ordinary circumstances, anyone can walk in there, sit down, and read, or write, or just enjoy the northern exposure. Surely hundreds of thousands of people have done so since the library's completion in 1940, although it's impossible to say exactly how many have come in here: this is an open-stacks library with no turnstile, a genuinely public place. It was a project of the Public Works Administration (PWA), established in 1933 as one of the earliest agencies of the New Deal created by an administration that would build libraries to save books at a time when the Nazis were burning or banning them. Eventually, the PWA published a glossy, beautifully illustrated volume of its achievements that begins with the words, "Men build temples to the things they love," and—setting aside the exclusionary language; men are surely not the only creatures so inspired to construction—you might agree with the sentiment if you were to stand in this reading room. It is a temple to books and the love of reading, and it is a place open to all who share that love—ordinarily.[2]

As I write now, you cannot visit it, nor can I, and I cannot say when either of us might again be able to: like so many of the nation's shared spaces, it has been shut in the interest of public safety. To prevent the spread of the novel coronavirus that causes COVID-19, states and municipalities around the country in 2020 urged Americans to keep away from the places where we ordinarily congregate. Forced to retreat into our homes we—at least for the time being—surrendered access to our temples. Perhaps, like me, during this time you were suddenly able to feel keenly how precious these public things were, having lost them even momentarily. Parks, libraries, gardens, swimming pools, sidewalks, airports, seaports, schools, stadiums—all these things, suddenly shut, constituted the public sphere that Americans built for themselves under the New Deal.

My brother was going to take his family to visit our parents in Florida over spring break; they would have flown into Tampa International Airport, where a series of murals depicts the history of flight—murals commissioned by the Federal Art Project of the New Deal in 1939; it was part of the Works Progress Administration (WPA). That did not happen, nor did other Americans' planned trips to state and national parks given shape and structure by the workers of the Civilian Conservation Corps (CCC).

But my parents, like millions of Americans, were still able, sheltering in their homes, to draw old-age pensions, just as millions of Americans filed for unemployment insurance—both legacies of the Social Security Act of 1935, a centerpiece of the New Deal. Stuck in our homes, many of us continued using electricity generated in dams built by the PWA. If you live in rural America, you may well have sat somewhere literally powered by the New Deal, perhaps by the Tennessee Valley Authority (TVA) or the Rural Electrification Administration (REA). If the local government telling you how to handle the current crisis belonged to a Native nation, it was probably legally empowered by the Indian Reorganization Act (IRA) of 1934; if you live near the range, the common pastures were set up under the New Deal grazing law of the same year.

If you have ever taken out a small-business loan backed by the federal government, perused the financial disclosures of a corporation offering stock for public sale, or if—right now—you haven't the slightest worry that the bank where you have parked your savings will block your access to your money, crisis or no, then you have benefited from the New Deal. As indeed you have if you have ever earned the minimum wage, drawn disability insurance, or joined a labor union. Even if you live outside the United States, you are subject to the New Deal's institutional legacy in the form of the organizations that regulate global finance and trade and seek to protect the international laws of human rights.

Sometimes we suffer, of course, from the New Deal's failings, particularly its leaders' willingness to bow to racism. If you are a Japanese American, it is quite possible someone in your family was imprisoned without trial in a camp built by the WPA during the Second World War. If you are a black American who lives in a neighborhood with inordinately high pollution and historically low homeownership rates because residents have found it difficult, if not impossible, to take out a mortgage, that is partly a result of the New Deal too. And if you are such a black American, and voters in your family continued thereafter to cast ballots for the Democratic Party because they believed that, however bigoted it was, it was better than the alternative, that too is a result of the New Deal—because the 1930s marked the beginning of a historic shift that turned the Democratic Party into the party of civil rights.[3]

The New Deal matters because we all live in it; it gives structure to our lives in ways we do not ordinarily bother to count or catalog. When we imagine the end of the world as we know it, the world we are thinking might end is the one the New Deal built. And if we tell ourselves we need a new New Deal to build the world afresh so it will be proof against crises like this one and the others that plague our imaginations—like, for example, the anthropogenic warming of the planet—we are drawing inspiration from the transformative project of the original New Deal and its concern for the sustainable use of natural resources. Like the proverbial fish that does not know it is wet because it never leaves the water, we sometimes have trouble discerning the properties and extent of the New Deal because it is the medium through which we move all the time. We scarcely know where it begins. Which helps to explain why many of us, like that fish whose watery habitat is imperiled by poisons it cannot see, are not entirely aware of how the New Deal has eroded over the past few decades.

The book that follows offers a tour of the New Deal in space as well as time. Starting in Washington, DC, and going through Tennessee to the Navajo Nation and California before alighting on a street near you, it takes in various aspects of the New Deal as it goes, discussing how the program of the Roosevelt administration altered these places and the people who live there. Each chapter, in consequence, surveys a bit of what came before the New Deal, how the New Deal worked in that place, and what came afterward. The itinerary is representative rather than comprehensive; I hope by this method to illustrate how thoroughly immersed Americans are in the legacies of the New Deal, almost wherever we find ourselves.

The New Deal matters most of all because it marked a dramatic shift of power away from corporate boardrooms and bank headquarters, a shift that accompanied an unmatched period of widespread prosperity. This change proved so popular among American voters that for a time even the most conservative of politicians did not dare challenge it directly. As one popular joke had it, Republicans professed to believe that the New Deal was a wonderful thing—and nothing like it should happen again. Over time, the first part of the joke faded as the center of gravity in American politics shifted back toward the businessmen and bankers. In the 2020 debate over a relief bill in response to the coronavirus crisis, conservative commentator Lou Dobbs accused Democrats of trying to "push through the New Deal on the back of the American worker."[4] For a sizable portion of Americans, the conviction that the New Deal did harm to labor had become an article of faith—one that would have puzzled the American workers who lived through it, and who for generations voted Democratic because of it. But by 2020, even one leading candidate for the Democratic presidential nomination tended to fret over "the excesses of the FDR era" rather than turn to that period of Democratic electoral success for inspiration.[5] In this book, I will try to remind you why the New Deal mattered so much to most Americans, and why it might yet matter to their successors, that vast majority of the population today who do not share the view from the executive suite.

Iarlington national cemetery

A visit to Arlington National Cemetery, and a case that the New Deal matters because it gave Americans proof that democracy could still work in the United States and around the world

I f you find yourself at Arlington National Cemetery, you will of course want to visit the Tomb of the Unknowns and consider there, as John Dos Passos urged in 1932, how it happened that the generals chose this particular John Doe or Richard Roe to stand for innumerable unnamed bodies.[1] But then, afterward, you might take a few minutes to walk downhill, south-southwest, to a corner where you can find, not far from each other, the graves of William Hushka, who died on July 28, 1932, and Eric Carlson, who died a few days later, on August 2, 1932. Both men can rest in Arlington because they served in the U.S. Army during what they knew as the Great War, a war to make the world safe for democracy; both were shot and killed not far from here, in Washington, DC, itself, while serving in a different army and for a different cause. The story of that army allows us to see what might have happened to American democracy if the New Deal had not begun in 1933 and if, instead, the United States had continued policies akin to those of the preceding administration.

In the summer of 1932, the veterans of the Great War were suffering, like much of the country and indeed much of the world, from the Great Depression, whose destructive power had grown insidiously year by year since the crash of 1929, seizing jobs, food, and housing from millions of willing workers. The federal government, led by President Herbert Hoover and a Republican Congress, urged patience and confidence, asking Americans to pull together, and they did. But before long—too soon—Americans had spent all the reserves they had. Family savings, the resources of churches and charities, and the rainy-day funds held by unions and civic organizations drained with terrifying speed. The treasuries of cities and states ebbed swiftly away too, until all the old ways to survive hard times had dried up and gone. And still, for millions, there was no work to be had and no market for goods.

In 1930, the Republicans lost the House of Representatives to a Democratic majority, but little changed for ordinary suffering Americans. In 1932, the two parties agreed to an unprecedentedly vast fund that would ensure liquidity to the banks, in the hope that by safeguarding the wellsprings of capitalism the whole system could be kept liquid. But even if this new Reconstruction Finance Corporation had proved sufficient to revive the banks (which it did not), the many millions of people further downstream from the financial headwaters of the economy would have to wait a long time before any refreshing trickles reached their parched homes. Too long: Americans were beginning to die of starvation, though official statistics barely noticed it.[2] Nor did official data adequately count the jobless. So far as federal officials were concerned, complaints about the scope of the Depression were exaggerated—indeed, in the summer of 1932, President Hoover had quite persuaded himself and the chiefs of his administration that the nation was well on the road to recovery. Certainly the president could see no need to provide federal relief for the unemployed, veterans or not; that would be a radical, even Bolshevik, measure. When Hoover's specially appointed advisor on unemployment—Walter Gifford, the president of AT&T—told him privately that "there must be Federal aid for the unemployed," Hoover was "down right sore over his attitude," which an aide described as the complaints of "a weak sister."[3] And so Washington stood strong against the idea that it should lend the jobless a hand.

If you were standing in Arlington early on the afternoon of July 28, 1932—the date on Hushka's headstone, a date before so many graves were here—you might have heard the hoofbeats of horses. You might even have seen them come by, carrying mounted soldiers with sabers at the ready. Maybe you would have spotted their freshly appointed executive officer, Major George S. Patton Jr., as the Second Squadron of the Third U.S. Cavalry, recently given special anti-riot training, passed through Arlington on its way to the Memorial Bridge, crossing into the city to join the U.S. Army's move to liberate the nation's capital from an occupying force of destitute veterans who styled themselves the Bonus Expeditionary Force, or Bonus Army.[4]

The marchers of the Bonus Army began to make their way to Washington from the West Coast in the spring of 1932. In a speech to his fellow unemployed veterans of Portland, Oregon, Walter Waters called for a march on Washington. Their demand would be simple. The U.S. government, which in those days made no regular provision for pensions or benefits to the volunteers who filled its ranks in wartime, had promised those who served in the Great War a lump-sum payment, due in 1945. The veterans figured they would rather have it now, in this time of

Depression. A few congressmen, notably Wright Patman, Democrat of Texas, had already proposed bills for the early payment of this sum, or bonus, as a form of unemployment relief for veterans. Waters's bonus marchers would trek across the country to show their support for the bill. Like Waters himself, a former sergeant in the artillery who had not found success in his peacetime career, they had little else to do and much to gain from the country to which they had sacrificed some of their youth and innocence, and for which they had seen comrades die. "Personal lobbying paid," Waters believed. By truck and automobile, on foot and by rail they traveled. Word spread along their route of the campaign they were waging, and more and more men joined up. By May, bonus marchers had arrived in their thousands in Washington, DC.[5]

Sometimes, eager to get the marchers out of their own cities and states, local officials made provision to speed them on their way. Notably, the mayor of Cleveland paid passage for bonus marchers to take a train to Pittsburgh, thereby getting them out of his jurisdiction. And so the soldiers, group by group, kept streaming into the capital city. Police chief Pelham Glassford began to arrange shelter and food for them. The president was enraged by Glassford's hospitality toward the protesters who, Hoover believed, were secretly harboring radicals in their ranks. Asked by an aide if he would receive a delegation from the marchers, the president allowed that if bonus representatives could prove they were veterans he might meet them. He suggested fingerprinting them first, on the grounds that the army kept the fingerprints of all who had served. "I won't receive any Communists," Hoover explained; surely no genuine veterans could also be communists. By the middle of June, the president told his aides he could not safely appear in public. "The influx of bonus marchers . . . is sorely worrying the President," press secretary Theodore Joslin wrote in his diary. "The President doesn't want to make any public appearances at this time, saying frankly 'There are too many assassins here now.' " But, Joslin also wrote, Hoover was working on a response to the march with the secretary of war, Patrick Hurley. "He doesn't want to take any active part publicly, but he is pulling many strings behind the scenes."[6]

With the help of the Washington city police under Chief Glassford, the marchers set up camps on the Mall and on the Anacostia Flats, a couple of miles away from the Capitol, just across the Potomac. The population of these bivouacs grew past ten thousand and maybe even to twenty thousand; nobody was entirely sure, but certainly they numbered in that range. Determined to stay until Congress voted them their bonus, the members of the Bonus Expeditionary Force built a community. Some brought their families. There was a wedding, and a birth. They had barbers, a comedian; someone inveigled the donation of a piano so they could have music. Tens of thousands of copies of their newspaper, the *B.E.F. News,* were sold on the streets of Washington to civilians curious to know what was happening in the camps. Enterprising merchants printed postcards bearing photos of the marchers: a souvenir of the capital's occupation by an army of its own citizens. Waters had identification cards printed for members of the Bonus Expeditionary Force, issuing number 1 to Patman and number 2 to Glassford.[7]

The House passed a bonus bill, and the Senate took it up on June 17. Reports from Capitol Hill had it that opposition to the bonus among the senators, once near to two-thirds of the upper chamber, had fallen almost to half. The bill could possibly pass both houses of Congress. Hoover worried he might have to stand alone against the bonus, but he determined he would. "They can pass the bill if they want to. I will throw it back at them with a veto as soon as they do. . . . I'll have that bill back before Congress with my veto in ten minutes." Hoover need not have steeled himself so. The Senate stood fast and voted down the bonus bill.[8]

But the Bonus Army did not disperse. Waters kept the veterans drilling to maintain order in the camp. As much as any single person, Walter Waters disproved the allegation that the Bonus Army was a communist organization. He wore his uniform without insignia, kept it neatly pressed, and urged military precision on the men. As one sympathetic observer said, Waters was "a right winger, a fine American."[9] Some of the men in the camp called him a fascist; a few of those critics were indeed communists—but not all. An impartial observer could see fascist tendencies in Waters, who demanded "complete dictatorial powers" in his role as leader of the Bonus Army and who, mindful of the success enjoyed by Benito Mussolini's Black Shirts and Adolf Hitler's Brown Shirts, proposed reinventing the Bonus Army as a new Khaki Shirt organization, bent on remaking the United States by discipline and force. The Bonus Army's newspaper drew international comparisons to prove the veterans' importance: "For five years Hitler was lampooned and derided, but today he controls Germany. Mussolini before the war was a tramp printer driven from

Italy because of his political views. But today he is a world figure. . . . The Khaki Shirts, however, would be essentially American"—though similar to the backers of those strongmen overseas. The *B.E.F. News* had carried editorials promising "a new order" that would arise from violence. "The rivers of America will run red with human blood," one warned.[10]

On July 26, the president, the secretary of war, and the attorney general met with other officials to agree on their strategy for removing the Bonus Army by force. Summarizing this conference, one of the president's aides wrote, "Very shortly . . . the police will get busy or the United States marshal will take control or the regular troops will be put into action. There has been too much dilly dallying already. The marchers have rapidly turned from bonus seekers to communists or bums. It's time for determined action." Hoover drafted an order for a declaration of martial law, if it should prove necessary.[11] The veterans were not the only group trying the president's patience. The next day, as he told another aide, he "secretly" convened a conference of the nation's top bankers at the White House, warning them that if they did not instantly resume "their functions as bankers," lending freely to promote business activity, the president would "see to it that the Federal Reserve acted in their stead." The president was especially keen that price inflation get going so farmers could earn satisfactory returns on their crops. Hoover grew excited in castigating the bankers; he "read the riot act to them." As an admiring aide wrote, "My God, and people say there is no leadership in this country." The president felt energized by his newfound strategy of staging confrontations and telling all sorts of Americans, bonus marchers or bankers, to get moving again, to just get on with their jobs—or else. But the bonus marchers would face his idea of force first.[12]

Some of the marchers had set up camp in abandoned federal buildings scheduled for eventual demolition that were, for the moment, under the control of the Treasury. Obeying instructions from the administration, Chief Glassford warned the marchers they must start to clear out of Washington altogether, and that they must vacate those Treasury-run buildings first. Waters agreed to retreat. A sympathetic nearby property holder agreed to make room on his land for thousands of marchers and their families once they left federal premises. He might have had enough room for all who would wish to stay in the area. On July 27, Waters told his lieutenants they would have to leave their camps, one way or another.[13]

On the morning of July 28, Treasury officials told Glassford the abandoned buildings must be empty before that morning was over, and no later; police under his command should go in and force the veterans out. Wrecking crews were waiting to do their job. Accordingly, police and Treasury agents went to tell the squatters they must go. Veterans resisted, and police began dragging them out forcibly. A fight started. Some bonus marchers picked up chunks of masonry from the crumbling buildings and began attacking police. One marcher grabbed Glassford, pulling his badge off. The chief kept his head and calmed the rioters. But the skirmish was enough for city officials to tell the administration they wanted the army to come to the aid of Glassford's besieged policemen. The president telephoned the secretary of war, instructing him to call out the troops. Shortly after the administration reached this decision, fighting resumed between police officers and veterans. Glassford, on the scene, saw one policeman pull out his pistol and fire twice, killing William Hushka almost immediately and wounding Eric Carlson fatally. And that is how the two veterans came to lie here, in Arlington.[14]

The chief of staff of the U.S. Army, Douglas MacArthur, had worn a white suit to work that morning. In those peacetime years, he and his aides, including Dwight D. Eisenhower, generally reported to the office in civilian clothes. In addition to ordering special anti-riot drills for the troops, MacArthur had prepared for action against the Bonus Army by bringing armored vehicles into the capital city, ordering them to drive on side roads and instructing their crews, if necessary, to lie to any curious bystanders, saying they were driving experimental vehicles bound for a demonstration. Throughout July, MacArthur also tried to make sure that the army did not get involved in feeding or housing the bonus marchers: as one of his officers wrote, the general staff worried that if the army had regular contact with the veterans, the current soldiers might become overly sympathetic to the former ones, and one might reasonably become "doubtful about the reliability of the troops" if they were called into action against their fellow citizens.[15]

MacArthur was thus prepared early in the afternoon of July 28 when he received a command from the secretary of war to take his forces into Washington. Troops, the secretary said, must proceed to "the scene of disorder" and then "surround the affected area and clear it without delay." If the soldiers took prisoners, they should turn them over to the police. The instruction concluded with an admonition to "use all humanity consistent with due execution of this order."[16]

MacArthur got into his uniform and instructed an unenthusiastic Eisenhower to do the same. Rather than cooperate with the police, MacArthur simply told Glassford what would now happen: "We are going to break the back of the B.E.F. Within a short time we will move down Pennsylvania Avenue, sweep through the billets there, and then clean out the other camps. The operation will be continuous. It will all be done tonight." Before 5 p.m., MacArthur's men, led by cavalry and followed by a few tanks and then some infantry, proceeded from the White House in the direction of the Capitol, moving against the Bonus Army.[17]

The ensuing action was swift and decisive. The overpowered veterans retreated, hastened sometimes by the point or the flat of a cavalryman's saber and often by tear gas. It took little more than an hour for the army to clear the center of the capital city. By now it was the end of the working day, and homebound commuters watched in amazement and often anger. Some civilians urged the cavalry at least to "get down off your horse and fight fair." Others tried to shame the troops, shouting, "Yellow! Yellow!" After the U.S. Army's victory in Washington, MacArthur grouped and fed his troops, meaning to send them over the Potomac to clear off the remaining encampment of bonus marchers on the other side of the river on the Anacostia Flats.[18]

If you had continued to stand in Arlington through the afternoon of July 28, 1932, you might have heard the distant sound of horses' hooves and tank treads, and the cries of marchers and observers. Perhaps you would have seen the wisps of white smoke from tear gas and wondered what manner of battle was raging through the streets of Washington. Certainly the president and his staff at the White House could hear and see signs of the fighting, and had regular reports of the conflict from the battlefront just streets away. Despite Hoover's frequently expressed view that the marchers were dangerous radicals who would understand only force, he evidently felt some qualms about the violence as it progressed. He told the secretary of war to stop MacArthur from taking further action, and Hurley duly sent an officer to tell the general to halt. When the messenger delivered the presidential order, MacArthur "was very much annoyed in having his plans interfered with in any way until they were executed completely." Eisenhower later remembered MacArthur saying "he was too busy and did not want either himself or his staff bothered by people coming down and pretending to bring orders." Apprised of the general's attitude, word came from the White House that the War Department should resend the message. And so again a messenger arrived to tell MacArthur he should desist. The general ignored the twice-given order, and sent his troops over the bridge to clear out the Anacostia encampment. That evening, the smoke-darkened sky glowed with fire as the soldiers burned the marchers' bivouac, ensuring that nothing of value remained and that the retreating enemy, should they return, would find no shelter.[19]

Late that night, at around 11 p.m., with the military actions complete, General MacArthur spoke to reporters. "That mob down there," he said, "was animated by the essence of revolution." The president had to act firmly and meet the marchers with force, MacArthur reasoned; they meant "to take over in some arbitrary way," and "the institutions of our Government would have been very severely threatened." He claimed the Bonus Army's members had burned their own settlements. He said he preferred not to call them marchers and he believed hardly any of them were actually veterans. He said the civilians of Washington had welcomed his troops. MacArthur noted that he himself had liberated people in the past, but none had been so happy to see him as the people of Washington that day. "I have gone into villages that for three and one half years had been under the domination of the soldiers of a foreign nation. . . . I have never seen, even in those days, such expressions of gratitude as I heard from the crowds today." The operation had, in his view, been entirely warranted and an unqualified success, with no serious physical harm befalling anyone—at least after the army had come in to take charge. Secretary of War Hurley, standing alongside MacArthur, emphatically told reporters that the entire operation, from start to finish, "since the clearing of the first area, has been on the request and at the direction of the Civil Government."[20]

Few of these remarks were true either in spirit or substance. The marchers were mainly veterans. The soldiers had burned the camps. The operation had not proceeded under civilian instruction; to the contrary, MacArthur had directly defied presidential orders. Perhaps most important, onlookers had tended to sympathize with the Bonus Army rather than the U.S. Army, all the more so in the coming days when photographs and motion picture footage appeared showing soldiers burning the encampments, contradicting MacArthur's statement.[21]

The president supported the story of his disloyal subordinate. Joslin, Hoover's press secretary, warned him he would get criticism from the big newspaper chains, but he was undeterred. "Reds and the yellow press go together," he said. When an aide handed him a batch of critical telegrams, the president replied, "That's all to the good. Most of these are from radical organizations. Tell the press when they come in that I have received scores of telegrams from Communist organizations around the country threatening me and the government."[22]

Hoover ordered the attorney general to investigate the episode, and received his report on September 9. The findings included the false statement that the soldiers had not started fires, nor had orders to do so. The report emphasized the operation's success in clearing the city of protesters without casualties. Acknowledging that a tear-gassed baby had died, the administration noted that the child, Bernard Myers, had already been sick—although doctors who treated the infant told reporters the gas might well have hurt the child and certainly "didn't do it any good." The president released the report promptly, adding his own reminder, to the press and the public, of "the extraordinary proportion of criminal, communist, and non-veteran elements amongst the marchers."[23]

By then, aides and allies had begun to warn the president on a regular basis that he would probably lose the upcoming election. "The President was about wild today. From morning to late afternoon one caller after another . . . told him . . . that State after State had slipped away," Joslin wrote. Hoover did not want to hear it, saying, "If another man tells me today that I am going to lose . . . I will kick him through that door." He settled into a defensive position, striking back point by point at criticism of his actions without articulating a positive explanation for what he had done. As Joslin observed, "The President has the 'answer—hit back' complex as have few men I have ever known." The marchers, the president would say time and again, posed an immediate danger to the survival of the republic. Calling out the army had not only been the right move, in Hoover's view; it had also resulted in an efficient and painless removal of the mob. If newsreels seemed to show that the administration's report on the episode was willfully wrong—if Americans sitting in theaters around the country could see their unemployed and unarmed fellow citizens driven down the National Mall by troops and tanks amid tear gas and the smoke of their burning makeshift shelters—then clearly, as the *New Yorker* put it, "the Attorney-General is not a man who wastes his valuable time looking at newsreels."[24] No matter what appeared on-screen or in the papers, the president would not admit fault in his handling of the Bonus Expeditionary Force—and, by extension, in his handling of the Depression.

For Hoover's management of the bonus march resembled, in miniature and the extreme, his general management of the economic crisis. The unemployed veterans, he believed, should stop lobbying the federal government for aid; they should go on home or else to another city with a better market for their skills, and find themselves jobs. Those who refused were not doing their part to resolve the crisis and they also, perhaps not to a man but certainly disproportionately, were criminals and communists.

They deserved what they got. That none of the marchers died (except perhaps a baby who was already sick) at the hands of soldiers was evidence of his administration's scrupulous care in the use of force. But if Hoover had to use force to make his point, he would. There was nothing to gain by looking to Washington. Americans must better their own fortunes for themselves, in their own communities.

Hoover felt similarly about the bankers, as he had told them at the same time he was getting ready to expel the marchers. Financiers should get over their qualms and begin lending again, so that businesses could get on with expansion and hiring. The president had given them as much material aid as he would: after resisting it for months, he had acquiesced in the establishment of the Reconstruction Finance Corporation (RFC), whose main job was bailing out banks. But he was unhappy about the RFC and believed firmly he must not publicize its activities, lest Americans realize how wobbly the banks had become. "We can't tell the truth about the banks we help," he told an aide.[25] Whatever the RFC did, it was not enough, and by that summer, so many businessmen and financiers viewed it as a failure that Hoover had to offer its chairmanship to five different men before he could find a taker. The president remained firm in his view that the bankers should really get on with banking, not come to him for help.[26]

As little federal aid as Hoover offered the banks, he would offer less to ordinary Americans who had neither work nor a source of relief, as private and local charities expended the last of their resources in the depths of the Depression. But the president remained persuaded that for Washington to create a program of unemployment assistance would constitute a fateful step on the road to communism. If Washington were to hire people on the scale necessary to meet the crisis, perhaps by undertaking public works programs, it would require an unprecedented enlargement of federal operations. The nation would be "plunged into socialism and collectivism with its destruction of human liberty."[27]

In the decades that followed, Herbert Hoover and his friends and colleagues would periodically remind Americans of what they saw as the vital facts about the bonus march. The city police had failed safely to handle the marchers, who grew violent in resisting eviction. The president had no choice but to heed the request of city officials that he call out the army and when he did so, MacArthur's men acted humanely and effectively. It was the police who put Hushka and Carlson in Arlington cemetery; calling out the army had avoided further deaths. The nation had trembled on the brink of insurrection, just as MacArthur said, and Hoover's determined use of force had saved America from communist revolution. For a long time afterward, whenever a newspaper published an account of the march, one of Hoover's aides would send a letter to the editor reiterating the former president's version of events. Hoover kept a file on these items from editorial pages and letters columns, adding instance after instance that repeated his view that he had done what he had to do to save the nation from radical menace, and no more.[28]

When charged with a lack of sympathy for his fellow citizens and a brutal thoroughness in expelling them from their own capital, Hoover might have made a spectacular case in his own defense: he could have said, truthfully, that once he saw how overmatched the bonus marchers were by the troops, and how disproportionate the violence seemed to the need, he had ordered MacArthur to stop, and the mutinous general had twice ignored his lawfully binding instruction. Hoover occasionally thought about revealing this, especially when MacArthur appeared to be supplying newspaper columnists with the line that he had acted only at the president's insistence. "MacArthur had no responsibility whatever for that deplorable eviction, which was ordered, against his judgment, by President Hoover himself," a journalist wrote in 1934. The general "took command out of a high sense of responsibility, and to be on the spot to handle any untoward incident. A soldier's duty, that was all."[29] An enraged Hoover told a friend, "If McArthur [*sic*] is putting out this kind of stuff, I shall tell what really did happen, and it will do McArthur no good."[30] But the former president never did tell.[31] Had he done so, he would have had to call his secretary of war a liar for corroborating MacArthur. Hoover would have had to explain why he had never mentioned this disobedience before, which would have made him seem unreliable. He would have had to challenge Douglas MacArthur who, even if many or most Americans hated what he had done to the bonus marchers, was admired—by precisely those businessmen and bankers Hoover most wanted as his political allies—in clubs and boardrooms around the country, for his lack of mercy in dealing with the mob. For Hoover to acknowledge MacArthur's forthright disobedience of orders would mean admitting that what Americans were wincing at when they watched newsreels of July 28, 1932, was not a righteous if regrettable government use of force to repel a mob, but a lawless act of organized violence against unarmed civilians by an army acting outside government authority, a real—if brief—coup committed for the purpose of inflicting violence upon American citizens who suffered, as millions did, chiefly from joblessness and hunger. To say so meant admitting that the real threat to the republic that day—the genuine undermining of its institutions and an actual insurrection against elected officials—came not from the political Left but the political Right. Above all, it would mean doing something Hoover could never, ever do: adopt the view of his opponent and successor, Franklin D. Roosevelt.

Roosevelt gained the nomination of the Democratic Party for the presidency in the midst of the Bonus Army episode, flying to Chicago to deliver an acceptance speech in person, against tradition, on July 2, and pledging himself to "a new deal for the American people."[32] He was then in his second term as governor of New York, having sat out politics for some years while reckoning with the effects of polio on his physical abilities. Hoover had wanted Roosevelt to win the nomination, believing him the most beatable of the Democratic contenders. Indeed, in the middle of the Democratic convention, after Roosevelt failed to win the nomination on the first ballot, Hoover, noting that the New York governor could win if California were to switch its support to him, sent a message to an ally, urging him to lobby the California-based newspaper publisher and Democratic political operator William Randolph Hearst, putting the argument that Roosevelt would be the best possible candidate. "Thus the President is actually picking his own opponent," exulted Hoover's press secretary,

Theodore Joslin. This assessment of Hoover's influence was surely overstated, but the nomination of Roosevelt pleased the president who, Joslin said, "smiled more broadly than he had in months when he received the message."[33] Hoover and his aides believed Roosevelt was too weak, politically and physically, to rise to the challenge of campaigning for, let alone actually occupying, the office of the presidency. Roosevelt had made, they thought, "an outright bid to the radicals" in his campaign speeches, and when he went to the convention to address his fellow Democrats, one of Hoover's aides noted, "It has just been announced over the radio that Mr. Roosevelt is being helped to arise to his feet to address the convention and the whole country is now hearing as to his physical affliction." Taken together, Roosevelt's dependence on his party's left wing and on help simply to stand, let alone walk, would surely defeat him, they thought.[34]

Before a month had gone by, the Hoover men realized their error, but it was already too late; the Hoover campaign strategy consisted principally in saying that Roosevelt's New Deal would "crack the timbers of our Constitution" and "destroy the very foundations of the American system of life." Roosevelt's proposals, the president said, exuded the same "fumes of the witch's caldron which boiled over in Russia." In short, the New Deal was communism, or at least socialism. To adopt it would mean surrender to the same forces Hoover and MacArthur had routed when they put down the Bonus Army.[35]

Roosevelt, notably, did not back the Bonus Army's principal demand. In this he was consistent with his proposed management of the Depression. Asked in April if he supported immediate payment of a bonus, he said no. The federal budget should be in balance for that: "Books that are now in the red should be put in the black."[36] Roosevelt opposed direct payments to the unemployed on philosophical grounds. They created a merely "bureaucratic" relationship of the state to its citizens; as names and numbers on a roll of the idle, receiving benefits, they had only the most tenuous connection to their government and indeed might well feel alienated from distant officeholders who did no more than cut checks. By contrast, if the state were to hire unemployed people directly, giving them jobs of public value, supervising them in their work, it would create a sense of community. Government "accepts that task cheerfully because it believes that will help restore the close relationship with its people which is necessary to preserve our democratic form of government," Roosevelt's argument held. As in the New Deal more generally, the task before the American people was not merely to relieve the effects of the Depression (as payments would do) but to restore for American citizens a faith in, and a sense of connection to, their government at a time when it appeared to be in peril. As another essay in Roosevelt's campaign book pointed out, some Americans advocated dictatorship as the solution to the nation's problems, "but we do not want dictators in the United States. The other penalties of dictatorship are too high."[37]

Because Roosevelt's campaign for a New Deal was also a campaign to reinvigorate democracy and thwart incipient fascism in the United States, he found the eviction of the bonus marchers an especially alarming episode. The men in the camps had come to Washington to ask for help. Their Congress rejected them and their president sent the army to expel them. Still, the governor kept his concerns private—but vivid. To his aide Rexford Tug-well, Roosevelt described Douglas MacArthur as one of the "most dangerous men in the country." He described to Tugwell the standard set by Adolf Hitler, with his "unscrupulous use of specious appeals, his arousing of hate, envy, fear, and all the animal passions." MacArthur appealed to Americans who yearned for a strongman, who believed "democracy had run its course and that the totalitarians had grasped the necessities of the time." Roosevelt said that among people he knew—rich people, who came from privileged backgrounds and who found the mobilized people deeply alarming—such talk was commonplace. The "Nazi-minded" Americans were all awfully impressed with MacArthur's expulsion of the bonus marchers.[38]

Roosevelt's positions—against the bonus but in favor of aid to the unemployed, fear that the bonus march and the response to it might represent a combination of latent anti-democratic tendencies on the verge of erupting—put him in a difficult position. These musings belonged in private, analytical conversation—not on the campaign trail. He could gain nothing by discussing the bonus march as he honestly saw it. The Hoover campaign accordingly tried to lure him into making a public statement about the march. The secretary of the treasury, Ogden Mills, criticized the governor, saying Roosevelt was silent on the matter because he clearly had no idea how to deal with the difficult problems posed by the Depression. Thus goaded, Roosevelt scribbled some notes to himself on how to answer Mills. Under "Are you in favor of immediate payment of the bonus," he wrote the reply, "The answer is 'no'—but I wouldn't gas the veterans for asking for it."

He crossed out everything after "no," perhaps thinking it too inflammatory. But later in his penciled remarks, he returned to the same theme: "I oppose shooting veterans who ask for the bonus. We still have the right of petition in this country."[39] He ended up not breaking his silence on the issue even when Secretary of War Hurley joined the effort to bait him into speaking. Hoover himself noted that the Democratic majority of the House of Representatives had passed the potentially budget-busting bonus bill, while the Republican majority in the Senate opposed it and so did he. At last, former president Calvin Coolidge joined the effort to draw the Democratic candidate out on the question of the bonus. Coolidge declared that Roosevelt needed now to disavow the bonus bill, lest he encourage the belief that as president he would be irresponsible with the nation's finances. Roosevelt's failure so far to do so was, Coolidge argued, responsible for the nation's failure to recover from the Depression in the late summer of 1932. "While he remained silent," Coolidge said, "economic recovery was measurably impeded."[40]

With the former president speaking up, Roosevelt decided he finally had to say something. He wrote a letter to the *New York Times* indicating he would address the question of the bonus payment shortly and reminding the paper that as assistant secretary of the navy he had learned a great admiration and appreciation of the men who had served the nation in the Great War. In a letter to a veterans' activist that also appeared publicly, Roosevelt said that he wanted justice for veterans just as he wanted justice for all Americans: his policies would "restore the buying power not only of one group of people but of many."[41]

In a speech at Pittsburgh on October 20, about three weeks before the election, Roosevelt answered Coolidge, quoting the former president on Roosevelt's apparent fiscal irresponsibility and unwillingness to oppose payment of the bonus. Then Roosevelt quoted his own remarks from April, saying it would not be responsible to pass a bonus bill now and that the government had better balance the budget before it made such large payments to citizens. Throughout the speech he talked about how he favored reducing the size of the federal budget—that is, cutting "the ordinary costs of conducting government." But he made clear that his commitment to economy in government spending had nothing to do with his proposed New Deal. "There can be no extravagance when starvation is in question," he said, and while he emphasized again that he expected to reduce the "regular system" of conducting government and adopt programs "aimed at a definite balancing of the budget," he would always ensure that such efforts took a back seat to relief of the Depression: "If starvation and dire need on the part of any of our citizens make necessary an appropriation of additional funds which would keep the budget out of balance, I shall not hesitate to tell the American people the truth and recommend to them the expenditure."[42] The New Deal remained his highest priority, even in a speech otherwise devoted to budget cutting and pledges of efficiency in government finances.

Hoover would later complain that Roosevelt had shamefully exploited the bonus march in the election. "The misrepresentation of the bonus incident surpassed any similar action in American history," Hoover wrote in his memoirs, objecting to how

"Roosevelt use[d] the incident in the 1932 campaign."[43] But in truth Roosevelt believed the real threat posed by the bonus march—a fundamental threat to American institutions—was better left unmentioned in public. It was Hoover and his allies who tried to use the bonus issue in the campaign, repeatedly intimating Roosevelt would support paying the bonus and deriding his silence; Roosevelt responded only to reiterate his long-standing opposition to direct payments. He preferred work relief. And as president, he made good on his views, when the Bonus Army—or a version of it—returned to Washington.

In 1933 a group of BEF veterans and others organized a new march on Washington, and about three thousand of them arrived in the middle of May. Roosevelt set up a camp for them, including tents and washrooms and a well-supplied mess serving three meals a day. Most important, while continuing to oppose payment of the bonus, he offered to give as many as twenty-five thousand veterans jobs in the newly established Civilian Conservation Corps, a New Deal agency aimed at the useful employment of single jobless men in wilderness camps, doing upkeep and renovation of parks and forests. At first many of the men found the prospect unattractive and preferred to continue lobbying for the bonus. One afternoon while they remained in Washington, Roosevelt's chief political advisor, Louis Howe, asked Eleanor Roosevelt to drive him to see the veterans. Upon arrival, Howe announced he was going to stay in the car while the First Lady spoke to the marchers. And so, alone, Eleanor Roosevelt approached the men, who had lined up to get their federally supplied meal. She introduced herself, explained that she just wanted to see how they were doing, and began to talk to them about her visit to the western front during the war, when she accompanied her husband, then assistant secretary of the navy, to France. The veterans warmed to her and gave her a tour of the camp. She then returned to Howe and the car, and drove back to the White House, to calls of "Good luck!" from the marchers. As one said, "Hoover sent the army. Roosevelt sent his wife." The First Lady held a press conference to assure reporters that the marchers were harmless: "It was as comfortable as a camp can be, remarkably clean and orderly, grand-looking boys, a fine spirit. There was no kind of disturbance, nothing but the most courteous behavior." Within a few weeks, most of the marchers had accepted the offer of CCC work, and the bonus movement all but vanished.[44]

Walter Waters, the Bonus Expeditionary Force leader who had compared himself to Mussolini and Hitler and warned that the United States would need a Khaki Shirt movement to clean up its politics, did not accompany the marchers who returned to lobby Roosevelt for the bonus. "There's no need for it now," he said in a speech of 1933. "The B.E.F., though it did not get the bonus, served its purpose. We now have a government back there that is recognizing and attempting to improve the unemployment situation."[45] At least one proto-fascist was persuaded that the New Deal made rejection of democracy unnecessary.

The foundational belief of the New Deal was the conviction that democracy in the United States—limited and flawed though it remained—was better kept than abandoned, in the hope of strengthening and extending it. The New Deal would show ordinary Americans that their government could work for them, albeit imperfectly. And it succeeded: although the effects of the Depression lingered for years—long-term unemployment was, and remains, difficult to remedy—Americans came to trust Roosevelt's policies, to the extent that they increased his congressional majorities and reelected him by a record landslide in 1936. Roosevelt would increasingly emphasize his anti-fascism until, of course, the United States joined the actual war against the dictator powers. As a vital source of materiel for the nations united against fascism, the United States was in a position to declare the aims of Allied victory, and Roosevelt took the opportunity to say, as he would repeat until he died at the doorstep of victory, that the conflict was not merely a war against tyranny but a war for human rights—freedom of speech and worship, freedom from want and fear, anywhere and everywhere in the world. As Rex Tugwell wrote, "Practically every important phase of foreign policy . . . until the end of World War II" had its origins in the early years of the New Deal when Roosevelt already saw the world divided into democracies and dictatorships: "The opposition of the two principles was complete and final . . . to be resolved only by the surrender of one to the other."[46]

That war that at last produced that surrender would cost hundreds of thousands of American lives (in addition to vastly more from other nations). Some of these many U.S. dead would never return, lying forever in the soil of the foreign lands they liberated or defended. Some would come back to lie alongside their fellows, including the two victims of the Bonus Army eviction, here in Arlington.

One of that war's veterans who came back here later was John Kennedy, who served as a lieutenant in the navy. His father, Joseph, had originally supported the New Deal but came to believe that democracy could not survive. He opposed Roosevelt's willingness to fight fascism. "This war won't accomplish anything," he said. "We are supposed to be fighting for liberty and the result will be to turn the last of the Democracies into Socialist, Communist, or Totalitarian States."[47] The old defeatist's son was proud to prove him wrong, not only fighting in the war but becoming afterward an eloquent spokesman for the preservation and extension of Roosevelt's war aims. At his own presidential inauguration in 1961, John Kennedy would recall that his generation was "granted the role of defending freedom in its hour of maximum danger," and he welcomed the challenge. The United States, he said, must continue to stand for "human rights . . . at home and around the world." His words are inscribed at his gravesite in Arlington, not far from where Hushka and Carlson lie; the success of the New Deal in its fight against fascism made it possible for him to say them with conviction and for them to retain their persuasive power—despite Americans' checkered record with respect to human rights—for decades afterward.

2 the clinch river

A visit to Norris Dam, and a case that the New Deal matters not only for its legacy of public works but for its visionary thinking across state lines in ecological terms, prefiguring the benefits and challenges of planning for clean and sustainable energy

If you visit the Clinch River in Tennessee, you will probably see it running clear and cold, even in summer, its waters an ideal home for trout. Anglers wearing waders and sweaters walk in its shallows, casting flies. Many hope, though they may not say it out loud, that they will be the ones to best the state record for a brown trout, set here in 1988. But even if their catch does not break precedent there is wonderful fishing here, with plentiful rainbow trout, too. Much of the time, the current flows smoothly and slowly through the channel. The river's banks stand sometimes as much as seventy-five yards apart. Sycamores and maples grow close to the water's edge and thickets climb away from the river up the gentle slopes of hillsides in the valley. Some people who come here just want to look at the beauty of nature. Otters show themselves here sometimes, and blue herons too. Perhaps you might find beavers building their dams. But for all this idyllic scenery, there is nothing wild about the landscape. For the Clinch River, as it is here, spills out from the base of the Norris Dam, a project begun in 1933 as the cornerstone of the Tennessee Valley Authority, a major creation of the New Deal's earliest days. All of what you can see looks as it does because of human intervention in the valley and the rivers that run through it—and some of what you cannot see, down in the bed of the river, lies invisibly there for that reason, too.

The Clinch joins the Tennessee River not far downriver from Knoxville, where the Tennessee rises from the confluence of the French Broad River, flowing into the state from North Carolina, and the Holston, which drains part of Virginia as well. The waters of all these rivers gain force from their descent out of the Appalachians and the Smokies. From Knoxville, the Tennessee River then runs through the eastern part of the state of Tennessee, skirting the Georgia line—or, if you ask the legislature at Atlanta, running through a corner of Georgia; the boundary dispute has never been settled—before dipping down into Alabama. There it rushes down about 130 feet in elevation over just a few dozen miles, where it creates a series of dangerous rapids and hazards, particularly Muscle Shoals. The Tennessee River makes part of the border with Mississippi before heading back up through the state of Tennessee again to Kentucky, where it meets the Ohio River, its waters eventually bound for the Mississippi Delta and the Gulf of Mexico. From Knoxville to the Ohio, the river has run some 650 miles.

At the lowest point of the Great Depression in 1932, just before Franklin D. Roosevelt took office, visitors to the valley found it quiet, its inhabitants suffering hard times that for them began long before the 1929 crash. This quiet belied the valley's violent history. Some of the inhabitants' ancestors had been the self-styled pioneers who wrested the land from the Cherokee. Some still living had seen the armies of Grant and Sherman come through on their bloody western campaigns. Some families had surely supported the first Ku Klux Klan, which arose in the Tennessee Valley town of Pulaski; some would have supported its enemy, Governor William Brownlow, who helped ensure that Tennessee would become the first seceded state to reenter the union.[1]

Mostly, the people of the Tennessee Valley farmed. The watershed collected plenteous rainfall, both a blessing and a curse to the valley's inhabitants. Down in the fertile bottom lands, near the river, the rich soil served agriculture best—although equally, farms in the lower stretches of the valley stood more often in the path of the river's unpredictable flooding. For cash, the people oftenest grew tobacco; for themselves, everything else—wheat, corn, sorghum, and whatever vegetables they needed. They kept chickens and hogs, and cows if they could afford some. Such industry as there was in the valley drew upon the farms; there were mills for the crops, certainly, though not a great deal more manufacturing than that. None of this economic activity yielded much in the way of disposable income. Even before the Depression, per capita earnings in the valley were below the national average. With rare exceptions, residents lacked electricity. Nor were they likely to have indoor plumbing. They fetched their water from wells and used outdoor toilets. They had schools and churches, but so far as timely information went, newspapers usually came late to the small settlements. Some people did have battery-powered radios, but it was easy to feel disconnected from the rest of the country, tucked away in its midsection, far upstream from the nation's ports and their traffic.

Visitors to the valley in those days often noted they found the river and its tributaries muddy, not clear like today; erosion was visibly taking its toll. Some soil washed away owing to flooding and the rains, but much more was lost due to the accumulated activity of human inhabitants who, plowing up the ridges and hillsides of the valley, had first in hope and then in desperation farmed the nutrients out of their acres, "farmed 'em to death," as one resident said, exhausting the soil of nourishment and loosening it so it flowed in the channels of their furrows, propelled by the rains, to the flooding rush of the rivers. The river waters looked noticeably murky because they contained the Tennessee Valley's rich topsoil, traveling downstream, eventually vanishing forever at sea.[2]

Visionaries had seen potential in the valley since soon after the Civil War, recognizing in the rapids and the flooding a power that could be tamed and harnessed. A topographical engineer and officer of the U.S. Army, W. B. Gaw, wrote in 1867 that "to restore . . . vitality to a great section of the United States" was well within the capacity of modern technology, and that a thorough survey of the river and its tributaries would surely reveal "the insignificance of the time and means required for this work when compared to the gigantic results to be achieved."[3] But the resources never seemed adequate to the vision. In 1913, the only accomplishment in this direction was a small dam near Chattanooga, built by the Tennessee Electric Power Company in cooperation with federal engineers, to end the worst rapids there, regulate the river's flow over that stretch, and generate electrical current. Then the war that began in Europe the following year and soon spread over the whole world suddenly sharpened U.S. official interest in the untapped energies of the Tennessee.[4]

In the National Defense Act of 1916 providing for U.S. military preparedness, Congress authorized the president to acquire land for the construction and operation of hydroelectric genera-tors, stipulating that "the plant or plants provided for under this Act shall be constructed and operated solely by the Government and not in conjunction with any other industry or enterprise carried on by private capital."[5] The logic of national defense re-quired federal control. The U.S. government would use cheap and ample hydroelectric power from such a plant to manufacture nitrates, which it needed for explosives. The rapids of the Tennes-see River at Muscle Shoals in Alabama presented themselves as a likely candidate for placement of a hydroelectric dam, which would also render the river more readily navigable. The dam built there would not be finished until after the war had ended, but it eventually received the name of Wilson Dam and, together with its associated nitrate manufacturing facilities, formed a federal complex at Muscle Shoals.

After the war, the automaker Henry Ford proposed to buy and operate Muscle Shoals, thus launching a debate over the proper disposition of the plant—notwithstanding the provision in law that the entire operation remain solely in public hands. Conser-vatives like Herbert Hoover, then secretary of commerce, sup-ported privatization of the dam and its associated factories on the principle that the government really had no business operating a business. Opposition to the Ford offer, and to privatization of any kind, came chiefly from progressive Republicans, especially George Norris, U.S. senator from Nebraska. Norris and his allies wanted the Muscle Shoals complex to stay in public hands. The river belonged to the people and so therefore did its power. In peacetime, the nitrates produced at Muscle Shoals could be

used for cheap fertilizer to distribute to farmers so they could re-
plenish the soil of the surrounding fields. The power plant should
no more go into private hands just because war had ended than a
state-of-the-art battleship should be retired to serve as a merchant
vessel; after all, peacetime might not last forever.

Through the course of the 1920s, during the administrations of
Warren Harding and Calvin Coolidge, the executive branch preferred private uses of the facility. The secretary of war leased
plants at Muscle Shoals to the privately owned Alabama Power
Company. Outright privatization loomed as an eventual possibility. To forestall this eventuality, Norris and like-minded legislators
sponsored bills to ensure public operation of Muscle Shoals. One
of these bills passed Congress in 1928, only to meet its demise
when Coolidge vetoed it without explanation. Another passed in
1931, whereupon Hoover rejected it while making an extensive
and vivid case against the public operation of power plants.[6]

President Hoover emphatically told the Congress that had
passed the Norris bill, and the American voters as well, that the
question of what to do with Muscle Shoals was not limited to the
best use of a single federal facility with its dams and associated
factories: it was a powerful "political symbol" of a much larger,
longer-lasting, and principled debate over the proper role of a
government elected by a free people. Hoover did not shy from
explaining where he stood in that debate and what he believed
was at stake. He declared that public ownership of the means of
producing electricity would "break down the enterprise and initiative of the American people; it is the destruction of equality of
opportunity amongst our people; it is the negation of the ideals

upon which our civilization has been based." Not just the efficiency of a dam but the Constitution and the American national character itself were at risk if Muscle Shoals should remain permanently into public hands. After vetoing the Norris bill, Hoover appointed a new commission whose members laid out a case, once more, for privatization.[7]

The debate over Muscle Shoals thus encapsulated the contrasts between the candidates in the 1932 presidential election. For twelve years, the United States had operated under the leadership of Republican presidents who sought, often successfully, to reduce the scope of government activity. Hoover pledged to continue that trend. Franklin D. Roosevelt, as governor and as Democratic candidate for president, promised not only to halt that tendency but to expand the role of the federal government dramatically. The issue of public ownership of power plants presented him with an easy opportunity to illustrate the sharp differences between himself and the sitting president, and he took it.

In a set of speeches during the 1932 campaign devoted to public utilities, Roosevelt quoted Hoover's firm and principled opposition to public operation of power plants, and then proceeded to outline his own antithetical beliefs. Roosevelt said that Muscle Shoals and other publicly owned plants deserved a permanent place in the nation's economy. So long as the government ran some power plants of its own, it would have practical experience and copious information regarding the true cost of kilowatt generation. Government data on costs would provide a way to determine a reasonable profit margin. As assistant secretary of the navy, Roosevelt had supported the same idea with respect to federally owned shipbuilding plants. He did not envision a government takeover of the sector, just government participation. Publicly operated plants would, he said, "be forever a national yardstick" against which to measure the prices levied by private power companies. A public power operation would "prevent extortion against the public" by private firms.[8] Pointing to the St. Lawrence River in the northeast, the Columbia River in the northwest, the Colorado River in the southwest (where Hoover Dam was already under construction), and the Tennessee River in the southeast, he observed that in the four corners of the nation, great rivers, "four great sources of power, all of them controlled by the people," constituted together a potential "great government work" for the "development" of these regions.[9]

Roosevelt, wanting voters to know it would matter materially if they voted for the New Deal, drew a clear contrast between his position and Hoover's. Whereas the president said that publicly owned electrical power was inimical to American ideals, the governor declared that publicly owned power was only "as radical as American liberty, as radical as the Constitution of the United States."[10] Reelecting Hoover would bring continued efforts to privatize power, undoing the little that the U.S. government had done to realize the potential of its resources; Roosevelt's election would bring an expansion of public power. In choosing the New Deal, voters chose an expanded public role in making and distributing power.

Moreover, as Roosevelt's use of that word *development* indicated, the New Deal would bring much more than publicly provided electricity at low cost, and more even than using that cheap electricity to produce inexpensive fertilizer for the depleted farms of the South. Development not only entailed restoring pre-Depression conditions, it would bring modernity and wider-spread prosperity to perennially poor and chronically struggling parts of the country. A new and inexpensive source of electrical power would attract new forms of industry to the Tennessee Valley, and with those new industries would come more people and more occupations, more spending power and a higher standard of living. Further, the dams that would make cheap electricity would also turn the rivers into cheap highways, safely navigable, for goods to pass in and out of the region. The Tennessee Valley had already given up fortunes in timber, oil, and gas to pioneering businessmen who had left behind poverty. Federal investment in power and transportation would make a poverty-stricken part of the country into a modestly prosperous one, and an exploited landscape into one that showed the signs of good stewardship.

Through the end of 1932 and into the early part of 1933—the months between his election and his inauguration—Roosevelt consulted hydroelectric engineers about the potential in the Tennessee Valley. One produced a lengthy report on the feasibility of development there, confirming the president-elect's view that the region offered "an ideal and, at the same time, a very practical opportunity" for using hydropower to create "readjustments of industrial and living conditions," offering the people of the valley "greater home comforts" and giving the region "a better balance of industry," which would ensure "the retention or reestablishment of a substantial class of people" there. This poor region could become rich, its culture deepened and its population expanded by the use of public power for the purpose of regional development.[11] Roosevelt drew on the philosophy of his fifth cousin and uncle by marriage Theodore, who in his own version of progressivism tried to balance an economy of wage workers with "tillers of the soil," ensuring a better standard of living to both. But Franklin Roosevelt went further than his predecessor, envisioning a new practice of rural and regional planning, applying principles similar to those used in the laying out of cities and suburbs for the best use of available resources, so the people who moved into these places could sustain themselves in their homes, at work, and at leisure.[12]

In January 1933, still awaiting the start of his presidency, Roosevelt took Norris with him to Muscle Shoals to survey the site and talk to southern politicians about his larger vision for the Tennessee Valley. He described hydroelectricity as the basis for "one great development" that would unite farming, manufacturing, flood control, and forestry. The construction of massive dams would require thousands of workers, putting money in their pockets that they then would spend, spurring commerce in the region. The operation of the dams would generate power—not just electrical power but economic, social, and cultural power—for the valley. "With the help of Congress," Roosevelt promised, "we are going to put the Tennessee Valley back on the map of the United States."[13] The politicians around him were thrilled, Norris especially. Asked afterward if the incoming president would really be with him in this endeavor, the Nebraska senator replied, "He is more than with me, because he plans to go even further than I did."[14] Outgoing president Hoover shared the sense of awe, although not the delight: upon considering the "wild scheme" the president-elect put forth for the Tennessee, Hoover commented that if one wanted to stop short of rehearsing the "absurd" details, an appropriate summary would simply be, "My God."[15]

When Hoover's presidency ended, so did the effort to privatize power on the river. The Tennessee Valley Authority Act passed Congress and received Roosevelt's signature on May 18, 1933. The new Tennessee Valley Authority, or TVA, could use the government's right of eminent domain to acquire land, build dams and an electric grid, produce fertilizer and explosives, and produce, distribute, and sell electricity, among other powers and obligations—all of what Norris had hoped Muscle Shoals could do and more. The Wilson Dam at Muscle Shoals was incorporated into the new TVA system. The law also included a specific instruction to begin building a dam at a site called Cove Creek on the Clinch River.[16] By July, the TVA had its headquarters in Knoxville and its officers began outlining their priorities. They revised and expanded existing plans for a dam at Cove Creek, adapting the blueprints they had to conform better to the TVA's broad mission. Before long they decided to name the new construction Norris Dam, after public power's senatorial champion.

If, on your visit to the Clinch, you were to leave the quiet fishing areas in the dam's tailwater and drive up to Norris Dam, you would find that a road runs across the top of it. It is U.S. Route 441, which comes up from Florida; in "American Girl" Tom Petty wrote about how traffic on the road echoes the sound of the surf—here the traffic sounds like the water running out of the base of the dam. You can drive across the top of Norris Dam, with the vast reservoir of Norris Lake stretching away to one side and the steep drop of the dam's concrete slope on the other. Norris is nowhere near as tall as Hoover Dam, the 726-foot behemoth on the Colorado, begun before it and finished at nearly the same time; Norris stands only a bit more than a third as high as its desert sibling, rising 265 feet above the Clinch. And apart from the difference of scale, you might appreciate that the two differ in design as well. Unlike Hoover Dam, which bulges back into the water behind it, bespeaking the immense and constant effort required to hold the Lake Mead reservoir in place, Norris Dam looks as though it extends naturally out of the sloping hills and riverbanks on either side of it. This difference in appearance is largely the result of the choice and intention of its designers.

Although the Cove Creek site had long seemed suitable for a dam, the drawings already prepared for it by the Army Corps of Engineers prescribed a neoclassical colonnade, similar to the one on the Wilson Dam at Muscle Shoals, which resembles a Greco-Roman temple somewhat incongruously spanning the river. TVA staff swept this vision aside in favor of a sleek concrete wall whose contours continued the lines of the land around it. Norris Dam would become a monument of the modernist moment built, as the TVA came to say, by and for the people of the United States of America, beholden to no ancient style but demonstrating instead the integration of sophisticated engineering with manicured nature. The dam's principal architect, Roland Wank, ensured that the TVA would build overlooks for visitors so that the American people could come to admire what their country had achieved. Wank, an Austrian émigré, also used a method of finishing the concrete that would create alternating squares, a checkerboard motif adapted from Viennese architecture. In this application the pattern would hide imperfections in the concrete and also break up its otherwise featureless surface. The immense structure thereby acquired a humanly comprehensible scale.[17]

The TVA would build twenty dams over twenty years, and other agencies of the New Deal would build more dams influenced by the style. If you have seen some of them, perhaps you will not readily appreciate how unusual Norris Dam would have seemed when first built; perhaps you will simply feel that this is how a big dam should look. But the style of Norris Dam was novel, and greeted as such at the time, for better and worse.

In the fall of 1933, this visionary proposition began with labor in the muck. Workers built temporary timber and clay dams to divert the Clinch River, laying bare its bed so they could pour the concrete foundations, more than two hundred feet thick, of Norris Dam. The once somnolent valley echoed with the thunder of construction. Thousands of workers knocked wooden forms together, jackhammered stone, mixed cement.

Nor was the building of the dam the only new activity. To make way for Norris Lake, the reservoir behind the dam, the TVA would buy some 150,000 acres and displace around thirty-five hundred families from the basin.[18] Land appraisers for the TVA began traveling the basin in pairs, looking over a tract of land, taking notes, and making an estimate of value that they then forwarded to the TVA's home office for approval. In due course clerks in Knoxville would send an offer through the mail to the landowner for consideration. After a suitable waiting period, a TVA buyer would come to the farm owner's door, prepared to purchase the land for the set price. Most landholders took the offer without extensive discussion; there was no opportunity to bargain, and if they did not move, the dammed-up waters of the Clinch would soon enough rise over their heads and roofs.[19]

So one by one the landowners sold and, as permitted by the TVA, dismantled their houses, keeping such lumber and hardware as they thought they could use. Driving through the valley after the buyers had come through, a reporter saw one emptied lot after another, everything reusable taken off, with nothing left of the old homesteads but maybe "the weird front steps, standing all alone."[20]

Farmers who worked someone else's property—tenants—got nothing and took nothing, for they owned no land. TVA staff had neither budget nor charter to guide tenant farmers, though they could give referrals to other federal agencies charged with relief and resettlement. Even the landowners, who received compensation, faced considerable uncertainty and little assistance in finding new homes and work. After the long and difficult process of evacuating families, one TVA official wrote that he and his colleagues had to "agree that we have lowered the standards of living for numbers of families displaced by the Norris Dam development. We attempt to justify ourselves by hoping that the future progress that will result from the building of the dam will in some way enable these families to raise their standard of living."[21] They hoped that the good the project could do would ultimately outweigh the harm.

For those families that stayed in the vicinity, the New Deal had much to offer even before the dam was complete. The Civilian Conservation Corps set up a camp near the construction site and began sending workers throughout the valley. Some built or improved roads and paths. Many went farm to farm, putting in work to prevent erosion of the land that would remain above the water and under tillage, and building terraces on the hillsides. Alongside them, agricultural outreach agents working for the TVA traveled the valley looking for families willing to learn new techniques of plowing, crop rotation, and fertilizing. The volunteers, designated "demonstration farmers," would illustrate for their neighbors the worth of learning from the government men—who were, in truth, mainly their fellow Tennesseeans, employed in new jobs. More than twenty-seven hundred farms became demonstration sites in the program's first couple of years. Although valley residents and TVA men all had their favorite stories about stubborn hillbillies mistrustful of newfangled ways, in truth, as one reporter wrote, "There are very few so backwoodsy, the Authority men say, that they aren't willing to try. In fact, the thing spreads like ripples on a pond."[22]

Four miles from the dam, off the farms, the TVA even built a town of its own, also named Norris. It would house the dam's workers during the time of construction and afterward serve as the nucleus of a new community. The inexpensive but solid houses had gabled roofs, drawing on traditional local designs. Planners sited the homes on the land at a generous thirty yards apart, and plotted among them a winding, planted common area—a greenbelt—to provide space for recreation. The houses had telephones and the whole town had electricity. The standard of living was high, and so was morale, which helped to explain why the dam proceeded well ahead of schedule and with an enviable safety record.[23]

The New Dealers brought to the people of the valley an awareness that in exploiting their land for immediate profit, heedless of the effects on the surrounding countryside or the future, they had "sinned against the unity of nature," as TVA director David Lilienthal wrote.[24] Now, though, the TVA would bring valley residents together to cooperate and discuss their shared and ongoing interests. Demonstration farmers had personal experience of how the new and improved methods worked to their advantage. These farmers and their neighbors formed a community, and soon organized co-operatives to arrange the better use of their resources and petition the TVA's local officials to help meet their further needs.[25] The presence in their region of an institution with power to assist them gave the farmers cause to organize and reason to hope they would be heard and helped. Another TVA director, Arthur Morgan, charged TVA officials to fulfill all "the possibilities of personal, social, economic, legal, and cultural development" in the region.[26] Attentive to such a wide range of potentials, the TVA gave residents, Lilienthal argued, the opportunity to teach themselves how to govern themselves better. The Authority sponsored "a steady process of citizen self-education," he wrote. The same principle applied on construction sites, where the TVA formed joint union-management committees to ensure good use of human resources, as well as natural ones, in building dams.[27]

Late in 1935, with Norris Dam almost finished, the Scripps-Howard newspaper columnist Ernie Pyle visited the valley. He meant, he wrote, to examine the TVA and "give it the works," hoping "to explain the Tennessee Valley Authority so that a child can understand it." But he found himself overwhelmed by his firsthand experience of the scope of what was under way there, not just in the building of Norris Dam, but with respect to the whole valley. He had to convey first the emotional force of the enterprise before he could explain it. Like many Americans, he found himself dumbstruck by the TVA's power to generate activity as nothing else could in the Depression. He stood in amazement, watching hundreds of workers rushing this way and that, dodging trucks that wove among piles of lumber and steel pipes, making way for cement mixers and stone crushers. He saw how the men had strung steel cables across the canyon to shuttle material back and forth, how they had built temporary roads all over the site. Every so often, a mud-encrusted car would pull up and engineers wearing similarly mud-encrusted boots and clothes would pile out to confer, pointing and writing and calling out directions. Pyle looked down at the base of the still-incomplete dam and saw the flow of water already coming through the brand-new spillways as the Clinch proceeded on its way under new management. "There is a boom, boom, boom about it that gives me the same thing the rush of Forty-second and Broadway gives some people," he wrote. The New Deal's ability to put Americans to work with a purpose gave Pyle a heart-pounding thrill. In his delight he explored the corridors that ran the length of the dam's interior, marveling that it was no mere wall but a building with insides. Then he climbed to its top, getting down on his knees near the downstream edge, his hands finding steel reinforcement bars still exposed in the unfinished surface to grab so he could cantilever his head and shoulders over the edge, looking fifteen stories down the vertiginous slope of this brand-new machine the size of—and indeed, containing much of the rock from—one of the nearby hills. Americans had never seen such a mobilization of their fellow citizens for an aim so complex and so constructive. And this dam was only one of many dams to come among many other projects set in motion by the New Deal.[28]

Pyle believed this outsized ambition accounted for much of the TVA's appeal. He traced for his readers the extent of the Tennessee River and its meandering flow through the states of the Upper South. He remarked on the quantity of silt, that had once been topsoil, washing through its currents. "Don't think erosion is just some platitudinous New Deal word either," he warned. "It really is . . . one of those insidious things like T.B. that we don't take seriously until someone we know gets it." The Tennessee Valley had got it and was fast perishing because of it: "They say that in another hundred years all this region of the South would be like another Death Valley," he wrote. But the TVA meant to cure the problem, trammeling the river to stop its destructive flooding and schooling its human neighbors to use sustainable farming methods.[29]

Pyle tried to list all the TVA's various programs but despaired of summarizing the mission, making his final point "the word 'Everything.' " Publicly provided electricity, fertilizer, and flood control were only the beginnings of an agenda that encompassed all manner of improvements in the use of resources. The TVA "is, in reality, a program to help the people improve their general all-around lot in life."[30]

To an extent those ambitions would be realized. Norris Dam formally inaugurated operations on March 4, 1936, three years to the day after Roosevelt first took the oath of office. The president declared, "Norris Dam is a practical symbol of better life and greater opportunity for millions of citizens in our country." Roosevelt did not travel to Tennessee for the occasion, but from his office pressed a gold telegraph key to instruct on-site engineers to begin official operations.[31]

In the years that followed, the river's energies, pent and regulated by the TVA's projects, did indeed transform the region and its people. The TVA's new dams and reservoirs allowed control of the river's height and brought an end to catastrophic flooding, protecting as many as 10 million acres in the valley and downriver, around the Ohio. Together with the terraced hillsides, flood control stopped runaway erosion, and the waters cleared. With the river more fully managed, traffic on it and its tributaries increased in quantity and, with prosperity, improved in quality, carrying more and more finished goods. More than 1.3 million Americans used affordable electricity that came from TVA generators. Under the pressure of evidence from Roosevelt's public yardstick, monopoly profits in the electricity industry fell. With cheaper and more widespread electricity, more machinery came to the valley, and its manufacturing capacity grew twice as fast as the national average. Per capita income improved from well below half the national average to nearly two-thirds the national average within twenty years. With increased income, the valley contributed still more to the U.S. Treasury, shouldering a fairer share of the federal budget.[32] Later economic analysis attributed a substantial share of the valley's economic modernization to the TVA and its work.[33] More skeptical economists with greater confidence in the private sector sometimes said that market forces would eventually have effected all these changes without the TVA. Asked to consider this suggestion, one newspaper publisher in the valley replied, "Well, they didn't."[34]

A joke recorded in the South during the New Deal encapsulated the fierce affection the TVA and other Roosevelt administration programs won for the Democratic Party and its policies. A schoolteacher administers a sort of secular catechism to her class, asking where the schoolhouse, the road, the electricity, the jobs, and the elderly townsfolk's pensions came from. The children robustly answer that Roosevelt and the New Deal had begotten each. Then the teacher throws out a poser: "Who made you?" Flummoxed, the pupils shift and do not reply, until one little boy tentatively guesses, "God." At which point, a disgusted classmate says, "Throw that sorry Republican out of here."[35]

Norris Dam and the town of Norris drew early and lasting admiration for the novelty and elegance of their design. The pioneering architect Eliel Saarinen appreciated the affordability and livability of the updated American designs in the model town, citing it as proof that American modernists should look to their own traditions rather than emulate European innovators.[36] It was a lesson he and his son Eero applied in their work. Indeed, the European modernist innovator Le Corbusier drew inspiration from Norris Dam: he appreciated how this massive piece of engineering, whose purpose was to interfere with the natural progress of the river, nevertheless seemed to belong to the landscape and the people. It was, he wrote, "a marvel of complete agreement and harmony between man and nature," its design so unobtrusive as to make "the proportion . . . almost automatic. It is an edifying spectacle."[37] Even the conservative critic and poet Donald Davidson, who viewed the federal government with distaste and especially disliked what he called "the lure of maximum possibilities" that the New Deal represented, had to admit that the TVA understood how to steward the land and design a dam. Considering a motorist's approach, Davidson wrote, "The nearer he came to Norris Dam, the more the countryside took on the appearance of an amiable wild park which told him, without words, how Tennessee ought to look if it were benevolently protected from man's foolishness." The dam itself, he grudgingly confessed, "aptly fitted where it belonged, if one were going to build a dam."[38] Other conservative white southern men sometimes felt something of incalculable value had been lost with this transition to modernity in the valley, and would tell interviewers so—although their wives would sometimes remind them that they had not been the ones who had to keep the fires going and fetch the water from the well in the time before electricity and plumbing.[39]

Black southerners took a more mixed view of the TVA. For as much as the TVA did to change the Tennessee Valley, it left the region's racism largely untouched and in some ways reinforced it. The relocation officers who went through the areas about to be flooded would buy out black farmers as well as white ones, but did not give them even the meager aid they gave to their white neighbors.[40] The TVA's hiring policies prescribed employment of

African Americans in proportion to their share of the local population. Its workforce was therefore about 20 percent black in the vicinity of Muscle Shoals, in northern Alabama, and only about 2 percent black near Norris Dam. Moreover, the TVA segregated its worksites by race and tended to hire black workers into lower-skilled, and therefore lower-income, jobs.[41] The model town of Norris had no black residents.[42]

The few black professionals hired by the TVA found themselves in a difficult position. They liked the prestige and the pay that went with the job, and at least some of the time they found themselves believing in the TVA's potential to improve the lives of African Americans. Yet they also found themselves compelled to protest against its perpetuation of white supremacy. J. Max Bond, hired as a personnel officer specifically in charge of black employees, played multiple roles during his four years at the TVA. While doing his job and conveying concerns to the white leaders of the organization as well as defending it to black critics who targeted him for complaint, he also privately encouraged and abetted NAACP investigations of the project, which led to heightened press scrutiny of its racist practices. This simultaneous support and critique took its toll on black officials; as Bond wrote, his department achieved at best partial successes on behalf of black workers, but what advances he and his staff had achieved, they had "accomplished under conditions that under ordinary circumstances would have resulted in the complete frustration of these employees."[43]

J. Saunders Redding, an eminent black literary scholar, traveled to TVA country, a little after Pyle and about the same time as Davidson, to take his own look at the territory. He met a personnel officer with views and concerns similar to Bond's. White laborers were getting better work—and with it, better training—than black workers. "Democracy's taking an awful beating on the T.V.A.," he said, venting his frustrations to Redding. And yet, he concluded, "The funny thing about it is, I believe in democracy. . . . I'm not discouraged, and I tell my men so. But I get damned embarrassed sometimes." The embarrassment was possible only because he did, despite everything, continue to believe in the possibility of the program, in part because what it had delivered was better than what black southerners had experienced before 1933. As Redding wrote on looking at the black workers' housing, it was "far better equipped" than other working-class black housing he had seen; "their poor little was the greatest plenty they had ever known."[44]

On its own publicly stated terms, the TVA became such a success so soon that officials in other river watersheds around the country began asking Washington to establish their own versions. Roosevelt had originally encouraged such thinking, as indeed had some of his advisors. In 1934, Rex Tugwell recorded in his diary a conversation with Roosevelt about establishing other regional authorities similar to the TVA. "I would like to go ahead with other Authorities faster than we are," Tugwell wrote. "The President is clearly preparing for it and has a regional set-up for the whole country in mind."[45]

Then, in February 1935, within a few months of that discussion, a federal judge cast doubt on the whole project of federally operated electrical power plants. In a case regarding the Muscle Shoals plant, Judge W. I. Grubb of a federal district court in Alabama ruled that the federal government could not legally compete with private utilities, and enjoined it from dispensing funds for that purpose. "The effect of the injunction is to practically nullify the entire TVA Act," George Norris said. Norris and other New Dealers pledged to defend the power program from judicial erosion.[46]

But soon, as cases reached the Supreme Court, it began to appear that Roosevelt's allies were making these pledges in vain. Justices began nullifying major New Deal measures, declaring laws invalid for overstepping constitutional limits on federal power. The Court disposed of the National Recovery Administration (NRA) in May 1935. The TVA looked as though it might fall too. In September, Tugwell wrote in his diary, "The outlook for a constitutional struggle, which must come, is dark."[47] In January 1936, the justices struck down the Agricultural Adjustment Act. As TVA director David Lilienthal later wrote, "I had completely resigned myself to a bad decision, only holding out hope that we would have some crumb of comfort in that unlike AAA and NRA we would not be swept completely out to sea, bag and baggage."[48] The director of the Bureau of the Budget counted twenty bills in Congress proposing different regional authorities akin to the TVA and asked the president what to do. Roosevelt replied that expansion would have to await a clearer idea of how the TVA fared.[49]

In February 1936 the Supreme Court pleasantly surprised the New Dealers, saving the TVA from the lower court's depredations and declaring it plainly constitutional. Provision for the common defense and improvements to the navigability of rivers clearly lay within the federal government's powers, and the power produced by water falling through a dam built for those purposes therefore was the federal government's legitimate property, which it might dispose of accordingly. But during the long uncertain time when the TVA awaited judicial approval, the project of planning for the nation's great river valleys lost political appeal. Secretary of Agriculture Henry Wallace and Secretary of the Interior Harold Ickes had begun to argue that planning should be national in character rather than regional—and therefore under the jurisdiction of their departments. Private utility companies continued to fight against an expansion of public power, and although their legal case had failed to kill the TVA, they still wielded considerable political influence. A Norris-sponsored bill to create more TVAs in other parts of the country consequently received only tepid support from the White House. Roosevelt instead backed a much less ambitious bill—what his aide Benjamin Cohen called "a pretty weak, mealy-mouthed sort of bill"—that set up a national committee with a narrower scope of regulation and planning than the TVA had. Even that mild effort failed to be adopted.[50]

Yet the TVA example of using regional planning to improve Americans' standard of living still had not altogether lost its force, and in the spring and summer of 1938, administration officials tried to give it new shape and life. In a pair of retreats in June and July of that year, one for industry and one for agriculture, Roosevelt aides convened policy makers from various departments and agencies to discuss how to move the New Deal forward.

So far as the industrial sector went, Roosevelt's advisors plainly felt that the Supreme Court had permanently stopped them from establishing any effective planning or regulation. Moreover, they believed they had learned from bitter experience that if they tried to regulate industry rather than simply run it, "the regulated industries would come to dominate their regulators." Having learned that industrial regulation was vulnerable to attack from both the bench and the corporate board, they proposed instead to empower consumers by two methods. They would attack private monopoly power where they could, and otherwise they would boost the economy when necessary through fiscal stimulus, using federal policy to put money in the hands of buyers, pursuing what became known generally as Keynesian policy.[51]

The agricultural planners took a slightly more optimistic view, at least in part because the TVA had survived the Court's scrutiny and had succeeded in providing a plan of general improvement for a largely agricultural region. At their retreat, they proposed that the Department of Agriculture set up a national network of committees at the county level, run by farmers, reporting local conditions to Wallace's office in Washington for coordination of plans at the national level. Wallace promoted the idea as a way of reconciling local with national needs that would "give farm people an effective voice in formulating, correlating, and localizing public agricultural programs."[52]

Had that summer ended differently, the U.S. government might have pursued a fresh approach to the planned use of resources for prosperity, trying again to strike a balance among local, regional, and national needs. But September brought the Munich crisis, which renewed Roosevelt's existing conviction that Nazi Germany posed a threat not only to Europe but to the world, including the Americas. If Germany were to sweep through Europe and take over North Africa, airfields in Senegal might become launching pads for assaults on South America, where Nazi agents already operated. A victory there would give the Germans a military presence in the Western Hemisphere and a way to strike at North America. The United States therefore needed a stronger defense—particularly, it needed more airplanes for itself and also to supply the western European nations in Hitler's way. With this logic in mind, no discussion of planning use of the nation's resources could proceed without reference to the need for defense against Nazism.[53]

The war, when it came, changed the TVA as it did so much else. Not far from Knoxville stood a major smelting plant of the Aluminum Company of America, which lent the abbreviated version of its name to the company town of Alcoa, Tennessee. U.S. government production of aircraft, already increasing even before war broke out in Europe, accelerated afterward and demand for aluminum kept pace with it. The need for electricity in the valley now exceeded even what the TVA's dams could supply, and in 1940 the Roosevelt administration authorized the TVA to construct the first of its nonhydroelectric generating facilities, a coal-fired plant using steam-driven turbines, to supplement its water-powered supply. After the war, with consumer prosperity and the renewed demand for defense-related manufacturing in the Cold War, the TVA increased its nonhydroelectric production and became the nation's largest consumer of coal. In the 1960s it began to build nuclear power plants as well. The Authority's mission to provide cheap power, once only part of the "everything" it sought to do for the people of the Tennessee Valley, became the principal, if not the only, thing it did.[54] Begun in an effort to make the use of natural resources more sustainable, the TVA increasingly became known as a strip miner and a polluter until, under pressure from the environmental movement and orders from the Environmental Protection Agency, the TVA began to invest in cleaner production. In the 1930s, the TVA represented how the New Deal could transform a region impoverished by human carelessness; by the 1970s, the agency and its valley had become an integral part of a nation that needed a similar overall transformation. The Clinch River and the Tennessee Valley as you can see it today—landscaped nature, stocked with wildlife, and ideal for outdoor recreation, home also to massive structures for managing the river—stands as visible if mute testament to the TVA's legacy. And so too does the sense of what such a mighty collective effort can achieve in one region without care for how it might affect others.

The river conceals in its waters one more legacy of the TVA's potential, something that you cannot see, even in the clear shallows: strontium-90, cobalt-60, and other unstable radioactive atoms—more than you would expect to occur naturally (though perhaps not enough for you, personally, to worry about). Some dozens of miles downriver south-southwest from Norris Dam stands another town built by the Roosevelt administration: Oak Ridge, Tennessee. Unlike Norris, it was neither small nor a model town. Begun in 1943, it grew swiftly to become the fifth-largest city in Tennessee while also, at least notionally, retaining a secret existence and identity.

Ten years after the TVA first began operations, John Merrill of the architecture firm Skidmore, Owings & Merrill was sitting on a train outbound from Penn Station in New York City, holding an envelope. It contained an explanation of where he was going. He had strict instructions not to open it until he was well under way. His firm was not yet known for its striking modernist innovations. The army had contacted Merrill to make use of his expertise in prefabricated housing. It had given him some unlabeled topographical maps on which to lay out a city and, satisfied with his preliminary work, now proposed to send him to the mystery site to see his town built. Once the train began moving and Merrill opened his envelope, he found that the site he had seen but could not name was in eastern Tennessee. The army wanted the place because, remote from the coasts, it was relatively secure from Axis attack; far from most population centers, it was nevertheless close to a sizable workforce in Knoxville; land there was cheap and easily bought but near to an abundant and reliable supply of electricity from nearby Norris Dam and the rest of the TVA's network. And the army would need copious kilowattage for the work of the new town, a confidential crash program to produce fissionable material for an atomic weapon.[55]

Soon trains rolled into the fenced-off area, depositing loads of material each day, some of it unrefined uranium from Congolese mines. Tens of thousands of people moved in to do work of all kinds. On arrival, they received a booklet enjoining them, "What you do here, what you see here, what you hear here, let it stay here."[56]

In the end, uranium-235 departed Oak Ridge on July 25, 1945, and arrived on Tinian, in the Marianas chain of Pacific islands, only two days later. On August 6, the B-29 *Enola Gay* dropped it in a bomb on Hiroshima.[57] Almost immediately the secret of Oak Ridge was out, and people knew how the energy of the Tennessee River, channeled through the spillway of Norris Dam and transmitted through the power lines of the Tennessee Valley Authority, had been transmuted into the most destructive force ever put to use in the history of war.

3 window rock

A visit to the Navajo Nation and an investigation of New Deal successes and failures in the arid Southwest, and with peoples who predate the United States

The Navajo Nation's council normally meets in Window Rock, Arizona, the capital city of the Navajo people. It is in the northeast corner of Arizona and close to the New Mexico border, about twenty-five miles north of Interstate 40 or, as it would have been in the time of the New Deal, U.S. Route 66. The council house is an octagonal stone building thirty feet high and seventy feet across whose raised vault radiates exposed beams made of logs cut from ponderosa pines in the Chuska Mountains nearby. Each of these vigas, as such beams are known in these parts, rests on the imposing mass of a sturdy buttress. The building's red sandstone facing matches the nearby buttes, which rise more than a mile high. On either side of the front door to the council house stands a seven-foot-tall wooden panel, hand-carved in low relief by Navajo artist Charles Shirley, entitled *The Livelihood and Religious Rites of the Navajo Indians.* The panel on the left shows a silversmith and a weaver; the one on the right a hunter after antelope and mule deer. Over the entryway, some more low relief carving in the stonework, effected by an unknown Navajo mason, shows a horse and a cow. You might therefore suppose that Shirley and his fellow artist believed the Navajos thought of themselves as artisans, hunters, herders, and ranchers. That choice would have suited the moment of the building's construction, in 1935, under the auspices of the Indian Emergency Conservation Work program and the Bureau of Indian Affairs, as part of what was generally known as the Indian New Deal, which fundamentally altered the legal and material condition of Native nations in ways that complemented the larger aims of the Roosevelt administration.[1]

From before written history, the Navajos, or Diné, as they call themselves, lived in the same general area as the modern Navajo Nation, though ranging over a larger territory than they possess today. Here over hundreds of years they have had contact and conflict with other peoples, these interactions shaping their traditions. Spain came and went, while all the time there were Native neighbors: first the Anasazis and later the Pueblos and the Hopis, among others. The land they live on is largely arid, fed by a single major river, the San Juan. It is a little more humid in the mountains, and there especially you can find adequate forage for herds of sheep or goats. The Navajos have relied principally on pasturing such animals since some time in the seventeenth century.[2]

Navajo dealings with the U.S. government represent therefore only a small part of their history, if a story of some recent importance. Although the larger part of the Navajo Nation suffered defeat and exile at the hands of the military government of New Mexico during and just after the U.S. Civil War, in 1868 Navajo delegates negotiated successfully with Lieutenant General William Sherman to return home, thus establishing with the U.S. government their continuing determination to remain a self-governing people on their own land.[3]

Federal law and policy toward Native peoples changed significantly not long after treaties like that one. Beginning with the Dawes Act, or General Allotment Act of 1887, the U.S. government aimed to break up the landholdings of Native peoples, proposing instead to allocate to each Indian head of family (as understood by the U.S. government) a homestead of standard size, 160 acres, and grant him U.S. citizenship. Lands not thus allotted would be available for sale to non-Indians; non-Indians could also lease allotted lands. The policy appealed to white settlers and commercial interests eager to claim land and exploit resources held by Native nations, and also to people who believed that individual property rights constituted the best safeguard of liberty. This coalition of business-minded people and principled adherents of individualism proved formidable. Within seven months of the law going into effect, the U.S. government had already applied it to six reservations and the legislation became, as one observer remarked in 1900, "a mighty pulverizing engine for breaking up the tribal mass" of land. It accompanied a policy of pressing English names on Indians for legal purposes, and of declining to recognize the legitimacy of Native governments and laws, as well as a generalized enthusiasm among white Americans for consigning the Indian tribes and their customs, at least rhetorically, to the premodern past.[4]

Like other Southwestern tribes, the Navajos never suffered application of the Dawes Act to their tribal lands. The dry country they held was suited for grazing, but not for dividing up into small farms. The Navajos therefore escaped the worst effects of allotment, although they were not untouched by the spirit of privatization it represented. Many Navajos, seeking better pasture, settled on lands outside the boundaries of the reservation and acquired homesteads of their own, and some railroad companies received land grants on the public domain running through Navajo country; both these piecemeal allocations of land resulted in Navajo territory that was not administratively contiguous. This checkerboarding created difficulties for people accustomed to letting grazing herds roam. Still, during the decades around the start of the twentieth century, when the U.S. government most zealously pursued the allotment policy and diminished many other Native nations, the Navajo population grew, from eight thousand to twenty-two thousand, and the federal government granted that the reservation should grow with it, from 4 million to 12 million acres.

Not only did the Navajo lands grow, Navajo institutions of government developed as well. Through the late nineteenth and early twentieth centuries, mining companies sought access to the resources beneath the land, including copper and coal. In the 1920s, petroleum outfits joined them in seeking permission to extract wealth from beneath Navajo soil by leasing the land for drilling. For decades extractive interests found it difficult to sort out these permissions. Corporations and the U.S. government alike wanted to deal with a single body empowered to speak definitively for all the Navajos, while the Navajos (like many other Indians) tended to organize themselves by local communities, units much smaller than the whole tribe.

Then, in 1922, a major oil strike by a subsidiary of Standard Oil on the Navajo reservation led to a more concerted effort by the administration of Warren Harding and its secretary of the interior, Albert Fall, to ensure drilling rights on Indian lands. Fall created a new Navajo council representing the entire nation. Each of six jurisdictions would elect a member—though the secretary of the interior could remove any member for cause and appoint a replacement, or appoint members to any seat that fell vacant, and the secretary's representative would convene and manage the council. Fall's orders did not establish an autonomous government. Moreover, his enthusiasm for turning over public oil lands to private interests, and his willingness to profit personally therefrom, became notorious with the revelation of his role in what became known as the Teapot Dome scandal. He resigned office in 1923 and would eventually be convicted and imprisoned. But the Navajo council he created functioned—at least at first—as Fall envisioned, swiftly granting drilling rights. Whatever the motives for its establishment, the Navajo council continued to meet and deliberate, creating a forum for discussion of issues at a tribal level. Notably, it retained control of the small share of profits to which the nation was entitled as a result of oil leasing, using that money to buy more land for the Navajos.[5]

Meanwhile, public opinion and, more specifically, legal opinion began to shift in favor of greater rights for Indians. The Indian Citizenship Act of 1924 extended U.S. citizenship to Native peoples, though it did not assure them voting rights, which required further litigation and legislation to sort out. The Indian Oil Act of 1927 clarified the tribes' right to control the leasing of all their lands for extraction of petroleum. And an increasing awareness of shameful material conditions, particularly poverty and poor health on the reservations, moved politicians and opinion makers to criticize the entire approach the U.S. government had for decades been taking to Indian policy. Secretary of the Interior Hubert Work commissioned the Institute of Government Research, headed by Robert Brookings, to study the conditions of Native Americans.

The Brookings researchers, headed by Lewis Meriam, toured reservations around the United States in the late 1920s, visiting Navajo country early in the spring of 1927. Observing a school, Meriam found conditions "most distressing." Sewers were woefully inadequate, and so was medical care. A measles epidemic raged unchecked among the children. Meriam spent one evening assisting a sick child who was too weak to get to bed without help. Moving on to another part of the territory, Keams Canyon, Meriam found people were suffering from an outbreak of smallpox. In still another region he visited, tuberculosis plagued the population. Throughout the Navajo Nation, physicians were scarce. Moreover, unclear rights to vital sources of water provided frequent occasions for conflicts that prevented the better development of the land. Meriam found also that the Navajos relied too heavily on their sheep for a living, and the flocks had already overgrazed much of the land. The area would need—as some residents told Meriam—considerable federal reinvestment to set the water supply to rights and allow the land to flourish.[6]

Meriam and his staff recommended these material improvements and also a general increased respect for the rights of Indians. The federal government ought to devote more and better resources to Indian matters, including medical facilities and staff, schools, and specialists in engineering and agriculture. The allotment policy, Meriam's report held, had "largely failed" in promoting "the economic ability of the Indians," and ought to be pursued only with caution. Even so, the report's authors endorsed the aim of the allotment policy, expecting that Indians would "be absorbed into the prevailing civilization" and eventually "merge into the general population." Improvements in material conditions and rights of Indians would serve to "expedite the transition and hasten the day when there will no longer be a distinctive Indian problem." The prevailing policy would remain fundamentally the same: "the allotment of tribal holdings will continue in the future."[7]

The Meriam report struck the incoming officials of Herbert Hoover's administration as a sound set of recommendations. They took seriously the idea that Washington ought to invest in improved sewerage and schooling on the reservations, though they could not secure much money for these projects. Also in keeping with the report, the Hoover officials continued to believe, as had their predecessors, that the Indian tribes should dwindle and vanish, their individual members assimilating into U.S. society. As Hoover's secretary of the interior, Ray Lyman Wilbur, remarked, the U.S. government should "make the Indian a self-supporting and self-respecting citizen." Some Indian rights activists continued to share these views, but increasingly, others did not, including especially a man whom Wilbur regarded as a "fanatical Indian enthusiast," John Collier.[8]

Collier began his career as a social worker who wanted to acclimate European immigrants to life in industrial New York

City, but he soon became captivated by the culture and modern living conditions of the Native American peoples, especially the Pueblos, neighbors of the Navajos. Collier achieved national prominence and an early political victory by campaigning to defeat a 1921 bill that would have helped resolve disputed title to Pueblo lands in favor of white settlers. After that success, Collier founded the American Indian Defense Association to assist in the protection, as he saw it, of Indian culture and property.[9] Collier believed that Indians did a better job of balancing individual needs and group welfare than the commercial and industrial culture then prevailing in the United States, and he hoped not only to preserve Native American societies from erosion but to allow other Americans to learn communitarian lessons from Indians.[10]

The notion that Americans suffered from an excess of individualism appealed to thinkers and politicians outside the small group concerned specifically with Indians: a faction of Republicans generally known as progressives. They remembered and had supported Theodore Roosevelt's presidency and his independent campaign of 1912 on a platform of conservation, industrial regulation, workers' rights, and women's suffrage. Supporters of the Republican Roosevelt rejected the idea that individual workers bore sole responsibility for their occasional unemployment, and believed that society at large owed its industrial laborers healthy working conditions, hours that left time for leisure, and a living wage, all as a matter of common decency.

After Theodore Roosevelt's defeat in 1912 and return to the Republican fold, many of his supporters found themselves increasingly at odds with their old party, whose leaders worked to shore up the Republican commitment to conservatism. By the 1932 campaign, many progressives remained Republicans in registration only and supported Franklin Roosevelt for the presidency. Early in January 1933, after Roosevelt's victory but before his inauguration, one Republican progressive, Harold Ickes, wrote to another, Henry Wallace, "Personally, I believe the Republican party is and will be hopelessly reactionary." It no longer offered a home for them. Ickes hoped for better from Roosevelt's New Deal: "If Roosevelt gives us a progressive administration it may well be that four years from now we will all be found permanently in the Democratic party."[11]

Within weeks of discussing that possibility, Wallace and Ickes joined Frances Perkins and William Woodin in a bloc of current or former Republicans in the first New Deal cabinet. The new Democratic president gave them the opportunity no Republican ever had, of constructing an administration that implemented their long-standing progressive ambitions. The appointment of Ickes seemed to observers to have particular significance: as Roosevelt's chief political advisor Louis Howe said, "Well! That's the first break the Indians have had in a hundred years!"[12] Ickes's wife Anna, who had an adobe house in Coolidge, Arizona, made a study of the Navajo, Zuñi, and Pueblo tribes in the area. She and her husband Harold knew and admired John Collier. Less than two months after Roosevelt took office, Ickes had named Collier commissioner of Indian affairs.[13]

For Collier, allotment of Indian lands was only a version of a larger American commitment to the ideal of liberty shorn of shared purpose—an embrace of the notion of freedom at the level of a single person, without much regard for the consequences.

Collier believed this idea had brought on the stock market crash and the Great Depression. "The country, in recent years, was brought to the verge of wreckage by planless individualism," he wrote in an essay shortly after becoming Indian commissioner. By contrast, he said, the New Deal represented a "determination to substitute conscious planning for mere economic drift in our national life," and moreover "to assert, as the measure of the value of each and every plan, the direct well-being of human folks . . . with the knowing and willing cooperation of the mass of the people of all classes." The New Deal aimed to establish, by democratic means, a peaceable sense of national purpose and a plan for the sustainable use of the country's resources. As the country shifted in this direction, so would its Native inhabitants. "The Indians, for more than a generation, have been suffering under a policy and a set of laws (particularly but not solely the allotment system) designed to force them into an individualism which has proved to be planless." Under it, reservations had literally gone to pieces, not only by the allotment and alienation of homesteads but by the careless overgrazing of shared but arid land that had begun to erode and wash downstream. Just as the TVA and related programs aimed to restore land to better use under the New Deal at large, so would Collier's office under the Indian New Deal. At the same time, Collier and his aides hoped to ensure that Natives would "improve their lives along the lines of their own culture and institutions," which would require returning sovereign authority to Native peoples.[14]

The new Indian commissioner did not lack ambition, and indeed he had a coherent philosophy undergirding his belief that he could bring planning and democracy to the Native nations while simultaneously respecting their cultural integrity. There was more than one way to be modern, Collier thought. "Modernity and white Americanism are not identical," he reasoned. "If the Indian life is a good life, then we should be proud and glad to have this different and Native culture going on by the side of ours." Soil preservation and production controls might be implemented one way by the TVA or the Agricultural Adjustment Administration and another way on Native lands, to the same end of assuring a sustainable existence for a variety of cultures and peoples.[15]

Collier immediately proved adept at adapting the New Deal to Indian Affairs. In his first week in office, he persuaded the president to establish a Native version of the Civilian Conservation Corps, known as the Indian Emergency Conservation Work (IECW) program. Its enrollees set to work building camps from local logs and, like their counterparts in the CCC, worked to improve the natural landscape so it could better sustain human use. Particularly among the Navajos, the IECW focused on irrigation and "every known technique of erosion control," including small dams and reservoirs. The program's newsletter, *Indians at Work,* proudly noted that almost all the foremen of these projects were Indians. The IECW set out to employ fifteen thousand out-of-work Indians across the nation, enrolling nearly twelve thousand by September. Of its seventy-two camps, more than a third were allocated to the Navajos. As would be reasonable to expect of any endeavor so swiftly set in motion, some confusion attended its start, and not all projects began smoothly. Still, in a short time, unemployed Navajos, many of whom had grown hungry to the point of malnutrition, now had useful paying work on the tribe's land and could afford to sustain themselves.[16]

The Public Works Administration devoted nearly $3 million for construction of buildings on Indian lands, and $4 million for roads. The PWA built the schools, hospitals, water-treatment facilities, and sewer lines that Meriam had recommended but the Hoover administration had not been able to fund. In addition, Ickes forgave some $12 million the tribes owed the government for previous public works on Indian land. Collier's Bureau of Indian Affairs became Arizona's second-largest distributor of public works money under the New Deal, exceeded only by the massive Hoover Dam project.[17]

In conservation work within the Navajo lands, erosion control took first priority. The Navajos suffered, as did pastoral and agricultural Americans all over the United States, from the effects of overly intensive land use. Just as the farmers in the valley of the Tennessee had seen their farmed-out topsoil wash away in the rain, and homesteaders on the Great Plains had seen similarly abused fertile earth blown away in the winds, so the Navajo herdsmen had seen their once-plentiful grasses cropped too short by their growing herds of sheep and goats, the roots of this forage dwindle, and the earth crumble into deep arroyos and washes that carried water away from their once-fine pastures. Game moved away. They could no longer draw sustenance from the land. More, erosion from the Navajo reservation accounted for nearly two-thirds of the silt in the Colorado River; Ickes declared that if erosion in Navajo country were not soon stemmed, it might fill up Lake Mead, the reservoir for Hoover Dam, within a decade. Even if this was an exaggeration, it illustrated the extent to which New Dealers regarded erosion in the Southwest, as elsewhere, as an emergency.[18]

Officials of the IECW, recognizing that the erosion afflicting the Navajo reservation developed from causes similar to the ones creating erosion elsewhere in the country, proposed similar solutions. Just as elsewhere, public works projects would employ Americans to dig out springs, build dams and reservoirs, shore up soil, and restore vanished vegetation. But also, just as throughout the rest of the United States, workers of the New Deal would seek to relieve pressure on the land by lessening the burden upon it. The Agricultural Adjustment Administration (AAA) would pay farmers throughout the nation to cultivate fewer acres, in the interest of conserving the soil; within the Navajo Nation, New Deal administrators proposed to reduce the herds that grazed on the land to produce the same end of keeping the earth in place.[19] They would also seek to replace livestock with less intensive herds: if you knew (as the saying went) which end of a cow got up first, then you knew that sheep took more grass than cows, and that any vegetation remaining when a herd of sheep had done with the land would be eaten by goats, so it stood to reason that sheep and goats were harder on a pasture than cattle. Working with the AAA, Collier got $800,000 to promote cattle ranching, buying stock to start herds on the reservations. Within six years, the number of Indian ranchers nearly doubled, rising from 8,627 to 16,624; the cattle ranched on Native lands increased from about 167,000 to more than a quarter million. At the same time, the AAA bought sheep and goats in an effort to reduce flock sizes and limit grazing, especially on Navajo lands.[20]

On the Navajo reservation, as in the rest of the United States, New Deal public works extended beyond practical infrastructure to buildings that symbolized civic pride: schools, gymnasiums, and other public offices. As Collier noted, the New Deal's overall devotion both to maximizing employment and to producing edifices that made Americans proud had a specific version for Indian reservations. His office sought to allocate public works money not only to produce buildings that would be simple and practical, and whose construction would provide work for the largest possible number of Indians, but also to make use of local materials and traditional designs. Moreover, Collier understood the construction of public buildings on Indian reservations as an opportunity to fill in vital infrastructure; it did no good to build a school building or government office that had no proper water, sewer, or power supply, and so the construction of such basic needs often went into the budget for Indian buildings. Collier also flattered himself that the results were aesthetically pleasing, using locally quarried stone or gravel, or adobe made from nearby materials, as seemed appropriate. In the process his office spent some $11 million for hospitals, day schools, shops, gymnasiums, and, most notably, the government complex, including the council house at Window Rock and the surrounding administrative buildings of the Navajo people.[21]

More than $1 million went into the construction of buildings at Window Rock. Upwards of five hundred workers at a time labored on the Navajo government complex, and more than 90 percent of them were Navajos. Using local materials, like stone quarried and logs cut from nearby places, and traditional methods, like adobe mortar and insulation, ensured not only that the buildings would represent Indian culture but also that, once built, the structures would need maintenance that Navajo workers already knew how to provide. As for the more modern elements such as electricity, plumbing, and heating, the experience of construction provided at least some Navajos with the skills necessary to keep these systems functioning.[22]

For Collier, the practical effect of the council house's construction ranked second to its symbolism. "The Capitol, or Council House, is Indian," he wrote, of Indian design, materials, and workmanship. It represented an achievement not only for the Navajos but for all Indians in the United States: "It should be of consuming interest to all Indian people, for it is a tangible symbol of modern Indian tribal self-government, and the Navajos are the first tribe to erect this visible declaration of their sufficiency."[23]

While the Navajos did indeed devote themselves to the council house and other New Deal public works, they employed the institutions of self-government in opposition to other aspects of Collier's New Deal. Navajos objected principally to Collier's efforts to reduce the number of sheep and goats grazing their land. That the erosion of the land was evident, all with eyes had to concede; that the erosion should be controlled, a majority agreed. Navajo herders even grudgingly allowed that they might have to graze fewer sheep and goats, and some did indeed take the New Deal incentives to shift into cattle.

As with other aspects of the Indian New Deal, efforts to control grazing had parallels in western lands outside of Indian reservations. In 1934, Congress passed the Taylor Grazing Act, which halted homesteading on the remaining public lands and inaugurated government management of federally owned land for pasturing privately owned herds. For this purpose, Secretary of the Interior Ickes established a Division of Grazing (later the Grazing Service and, still later, a large chunk of the Bureau of Land Management).[24] Setting up grazing districts and allocating rights of pasture required that officials from the Department of the Interior go out to the arid lands of the West and consult residents about their habits and the habits of their neighbors, conducting oral histories to come up with a set of rules that inflicted as little injustice as possible. On the one hand—as the new director of grazing, F. R. Carpenter, noted—one had to conserve the soil and reduce the number of animals cropping vegetation; on the other, one had to show as much fairness and respect for tradition as possible, seeking to allow herders large and small to remain on the ranges they were accustomed to work. In the end, though, Carpenter acknowledged he would have to make decisions in favor of some and against others: "Who are you going to open the gate for and who are you going to kick in the ear . . . and say, 'Go somewhere else and buy yourself a filling station or go into some other business.' " By consulting locally established grazing boards and working with herders of various kinds of livestock, Carpenter and his staff drew maps and set rules, but not without alienating—sometimes permanently—some of the constituencies they sought to serve.[25]

Saving grazing lands on the Navajo reservation would take some of the same skills but also require some different institutions. Navajos, like other westerners, had their own accustomed habits and territory for grazing, and some had larger and some had smaller herds; but they were, as a group, even less likely than others to accept the verdict of a New Dealer that they ought to get out of the ranching business and go open a filling station somewhere else. As a people they had fought hard and endured privation to keep their ancestral lands, and the range on which they ran their stock was Navajo land, not U.S. property. So Collier and Indian Affairs had to use different tools than Carpenter and the Grazing Service in seeking to save the arid soil. Like Carpenter, they needed to listen to local people who understood local customs, but in this they failed where Carpenter had largely succeeded.

Collier's office chose to reduce production, another method of regulating agriculture that was common to the New Deal. Under the Agricultural Adjustment Act of 1933, the AAA would tax the processing of agricultural commodities and use the resulting revenue to pay farmers to produce less on the simple principle that with less of any farm product, each remaining bale, bushel, head, side, or gallon would be worth more. By making less—that is, by reducing supply—farmers could charge more owing to the resulting increased demand. Production control proved popular among most farmers, who believed it was effective. And although the Supreme Court declared it unconstitutional in 1935 on the ground that the federal taxation power could not be used to regulate production, New Dealers reinstated the program on a different basis with legislation in 1936 and 1938. From then on, they would control production not with the unconstitutional aim of raising farm incomes, but with the constitutional aim of conserving the soil and other natural resources—with the additional and allegedly incidental result of raising farm incomes.[26]

The implementation of a similar program for Navajos faltered because of a combination of bad luck and poor planning by Collier's office. In the winter of 1932–33, before Roosevelt took office, severe weather killed some 150,000 grazing animals on the Navajo reservation. Nature had reduced the herds more effectively, if brutally, than policy ever could. But Collier's office, responding to the sense of emergency among Navajo herders, replenished their flocks, thereby re-creating the problem of an overpopulated range through federal generosity. Then the Indian office offered to reduce herd sizes once more, also through federal spending, by buying stock back from the herders with federal emergency relief funds.[27]

Collier personally visited Navajo country to make his case for reducing the grazing herds, explaining the need to preserve the land for future use. He argued that reducing supply would increase demand, as it did for herders elsewhere in the country. He also explained that relief wages from conservation work and other New Deal programs would provide new sources of income to the reservation, and that some Navajos who worked on construction projects would acquire new skills and new, more lucrative careers. He brought with him an aide who showed a graph with three lines: one representing the number of grazing animals (falling), and two more showing income from wages and from grazing (rising).

The presentation went poorly. One Navajo delegate, Jim Shirley, asked if the Indians would be allowed to speak at all. Another,

Henry Taliman, allowed that the graph might represent economic reality, but it failed to reflect the value Navajo herders placed on the independence they enjoyed as owners of livestock, which they would surrender if they became wage laborers.[28]

At length Navajos agreed to an across-the-board, evenly distributed 10 percent cull of their sheep herds, but many soon regretted it. The flat rate swiftly engendered discontent among smaller operators, who protested they were unfairly affected. Bigger herds could better afford to give up 10 percent of their sheep, perhaps choosing weaker specimens to surrender, while smaller outfits had no such luxury of choice. Once a herd fell much below a hundred animals, it might not be able to sustain itself, owing to natural rates of depletion. Chee Dodge, an eminent Navajo leader of long standing, warned that the program would not work for precisely these reasons, accurately predicting that the incentive to cull animals that were less valuable anyway would have little effect; the remaining, healthier animals would go ahead and breed, and the overall size of larger herds would thus remain largely unchanged. But Collier did not heed these warnings.[29]

The sheep-reduction program failed in the first instance, as herders kept their best breeding stock and flocks increased. Collier and his officials had to return to make further culls. The second effort at sheep reduction sought to leave small herders out of the equation. So did the goat-reduction plan, whose manager, William Zeh, planned to have the animals sent to a packing company to be canned for food. When the packing company said it had inadequate capacity for the goats, Zeh, in desperation to see the stock reduction proceed, ordered animals shot and butchered on the spot. In practice, prospective butchers could not keep up with the shootings—officials left some 40 percent of the livestock purchased for the reduction program as carcasses rotting on the range, an exhibit of waste and heartlessness that shocked many Navajos.[30]

New Dealers' ruthless killing of livestock to control production, and therefore commodity prices, was not confined to Navajo lands; to meet hog-reduction quotas the AAA had slaughtered some 6 million piglets in 1933, which Secretary of Agriculture Henry Wallace conceded was not how "any sane society" should behave. The United States had been driven to "emergency acts made necessary by the almost insane lack of world statesmanship during the period from 1920–1932."[31] But the killing of Navajos' livestock represented more than irrational waste. Collier's office destroyed a traditional source of subsistence for many Navajos, leaving some families hungry and even more desperate. Moreover, Navajo patterns of livestock ownership tended to run along lines of gender, with men owning more cattle and women more often owning smaller animals, especially goats. The reduction of sheep and goat herds severely and particularly reduced women's wealth among the Navajos. Collier failed to anticipate or monitor the consequences of this vital program which, he admitted, simply "rolled forward as a matter of momentum"— momentum that he, in his haste to secure results, had created.[32]

Stock reduction on Navajo ranges therefore was not only unpopular but increasingly seen as a threat to the traditional structures and culture Collier said he wanted to preserve. The policy fueled resentment of John Collier and all his proposals—

which was unfortunate for him, because he had a major new plan in the works for which he desperately wanted Navajos' approval.

Early in 1934, Collier hosted a conference of Indian activists in Washington, DC, to discuss priorities for reforming policy toward Native peoples. The discussion sessions ranged widely and lasted much of a day. At the end, participants agreed that their first priority should be repeal and, to the extent possible, reversal of the allotment policy: rather than continue to distribute Indian lands to individual owners, the federal government should cease doing so and enable Indian peoples to reclaim, where possible, land for common use such as grazing. To enable this reconsolidation of tribal lands, the conference members agreed also that the United States should recognize the right of Indians to organize their own governments—in due course, all the sovereign powers then exercised by the United States on tribal lands should revert to Indian institutions. As one delegate remarked, to his knowledge "this occasion was the first on record where a government official specifically and unequivocally agreed to the diminution of his own power and prerogatives." But that was the logical conclusion of Collier's policy: the Indian Office should dwindle, and its powers should go instead to the Indians themselves.[33]

Collier asked lawyers for the Department of the Interior to draw up a bill embodying the conference's principles, and by mid-February he got the measure introduced in Congress by Representative Edgar Howard of Nebraska and Senator Burton Wheeler of Montana. The Wheeler-Howard Bill was Collier's measure; Wheeler himself would claim he had not read it before introducing it, and indeed would later oppose it.[34]

To secure Native support, Collier called a series of congresses among Indian nations to garner opinions. Initial responses were not encouraging. A number of individual Indians and Indian organizations regarded the reestablishment of tribal ownership, after almost half a century of privatization, as a step backward, pushing Native peoples out of modern life and "back to the blanket," as the expression had it. The reservation could become a racially segregated community. Some critics, like Joe Irving of the Crow, regarded the conference proposals as "socialist."[35]

Collier continued to travel Indian country seeking support. The bill included a provision mandating that each of the Native nations vote on it and that it would not apply to any tribe in which a majority voted against it. He returned to Washington believing he had secured widespread support, only to find shortly afterward that one of the associations that had participated in his original conference had decided to oppose his program. The Indian Rights Association rejected the Wheeler-Howard bill for promoting "segregation" and argued that "the amalgamation of the Indian with the white race in the United States," however one felt about it, had become inevitable.[36]

In the end, despite Wheeler's defection and other opposition, Collier could claim that a majority of Indians and Indian tribes supported the law. Within a decade, nearly a hundred Indian communities of various sizes would use provisions of the law to establish a new legal basis for self-government. But the largest single tribe in the United States, the Navajos, did not welcome reorganization.

Publicly, the principal Navajo opponent of Wheeler-Howard was Jacob C. Morgan, an advocate of assimilation who feared that Collier's policies, by confining Indians to their reservations, would deprive them of the chance to gain the benefits offered by white society. Morgan himself had attended a boarding school in Colorado, where he had become a Christian while earning his diploma. Coming back to Navajo country, he became a leader of the Returned Students Association, representing others who had got their education off the reservation and believed firmly in the value of such a culturally broadening experience. Perhaps nothing illustrated the politics of the Returned Students Association so well as its custom of celebrating the anniversary of the Dawes General Allotment Act as a holiday. The association represented a politically successful faction within the Navajo Nation at the start of the New Deal, as five of its candidates won election to the twelve-member tribal council in 1933.[37]

Morgan campaigned energetically against Navajo support of the Wheeler-Howard bill in the 1935 referendum, on the ground that it would isolate Indians and thus "wreck the future possibilities of the mass of now uneducated people." He accused Collier of wanting to preserve the Navajos as a sideshow attraction, a "monkey show" for the entertainment of white tourists.[38]

Morgan's success in whipping support against Collier probably had more to do with anger at the livestock-reduction program than with firmly held opinions in favor of assimilation. As one Navajo sheepherder, Mary Chischillie, would say, she understood the referendum as a question of whether or not she wanted to keep her flock. In the end, Navajos narrowly voted to reject Wheeler-Howard on June 14 and 15, 1935, "in an election that was far from being a legal one," as an opponent of the Wheeler-Howard plan alleged; the ballots were supposed to be secret and they were not, allowing a considerable amount of peer pressure.[39] Navajos split openly and bitterly over the measure, exercising their right to self-determination by rejecting a law that was supposed to guarantee just that.[40]

Not long afterward, Collier's office found an opportunity to reorganize the Navajo tribal council anyway. The old council had ceased to meet and in 1937, arguing that the Department of the Interior had organized the previous council and therefore could set up a new one, officials established regulations for a government in the new complex at Window Rock. Under election rules established by Secretary of the Interior Ickes, Navajos voted for a new tribal chairman in 1938; Jacob C. Morgan handily won the election. Morgan's inaugural address pledged a new era of conciliation among factions and with the government. Morgan worked with the Indian office to establish local industries, including a sawmill and a flour mill. His administration continued to negotiate stock-reduction targets.[41]

Eventually, over the course of decades, Navajos would acquire control of grazing management themselves; herds of sheep and goats would remain smaller than they had been in 1933. The improvement of hospitals, water treatment, and sewerage led to a decline of infant mortality for the Navajos and for Indians more generally, whose populations began to increase more rapidly.

With the enforced and unwelcome decline of herding and the New Deal's provision of public works projects and local industry, the number of Navajos working for wages increased approximately tenfold. And on reservations, as on the range, the New Deal brought an end to policies that promoted the privatization of lands. It became one of the factors helping to set the Native nations on the path to the greater self-government and autonomy they enjoy today.[42]

Yet the intransigence of John Collier—driven, often mystical, self-righteous— became the singular fact of the Indian New Deal in memory. Temperamentally, Collier seemed unable to accept guidance from the people in his jurisdiction. One Navajo woman told an interviewer in 1940, "I really hate John Collier. . . . I could even kill him myself just like I could kill a mad dog."[43] Despite his insistence that there was more than one way to be modern, and that Indians—principally, he hoped, Navajos—would find their own path to a modern society that might flourish alongside the mainstream of the United States, his policies had dismantled traditional ways of life and set Navajos ruthlessly on the road to a wage economy that looked much like any other in America, only poorer. Navajos continued to try to establish local industry on their own land, only to meet criticism from white opinion makers in the Southwest that their proposals for taxation and establishment of publicly sponsored businesses resembled Soviet forms of development.[44]

The New Deal helped dozens of Native nations inaugurate a transition to more effective autonomous government. And, despite the difficulties involved, the New Deal served that purpose for the Navajos, too, with a massive influx of often-grand public works and the consolidation of a capital at Window Rock. For all that the Roosevelt administration created and used new forms of federal authority, in the case of the Indian New Deal, as in many others, it wielded these instruments to empower local communities. Sometimes, as with the Navajos, this reinvigoration of democracy meant empowering communities to declare how inadequate some aspects of the New Deal had proved.

4 hunters point

A visit to a neighborhood on San Francisco Bay, a region transformed by the New Deal in a series of ways that especially affected African Americans

From Hunters Point in San Francisco, at a spot not far from where Candlestick Park stadium used to be, you can make out a splendid view of the city's downtown, a prospect that includes a number of major New Deal landmarks. You can readily spot the gray towers of the Bay Bridge that support a suspension span as part of the raised highway stretching over the water from the San Francisco peninsula across to Oakland, finished in 1936 and built as a project of the Public Works Administration. On its way across the water, the Bay Bridge passes close by Treasure Island, a man-made bit of land dredged up for the purpose of building an airport for the city, a project of the Works Progress Administration. Treasure Island became the site of the Golden Gate International Exposition of 1939, whose buildings and landscapes, including the spectacular Tower of the Sun, were projects of the PWA and WPA—as were the highways and hangars of the eventual San Francisco Municipal Airport, constructed on a small airfield called Mills just south of the city. From this spot, on Hunters Point, you can often see passenger jets flying to and from that same site, at what is now San Francisco International Airport (SFO). Off to the left of the Bay Bridge, north of the city, stand the orange towers of the Golden Gate Bridge, finished in 1937, stretching north across the entrance of the bay to

Marin; its approaches and lighting were built by laborers of the WPA, too. The city as it is today, a peninsula served by bridges that allow automobiles—too many, to be sure—to pass in and out, by an airport where cross-country and transoceanic flights can take off and land, is a creation of the New Deal.[1]

So too are some of its more modest civic buildings. Off to the left, and much closer than downtown—only about two miles away—is the Sunshine School, a campus standing around an open patio playground. The facility, a PWA project built in 1937, was specially designed to provide accessibility to people using wheelchairs, and to support the treatment and education of children with disabilities or chronic illnesses.[2]

Out of sight from here, but on the waterfront between the Bay Bridge and the Golden Gate Bridge, stands Aquatic Park, protected by a long seawall supporting a promenade. The area was completed as a WPA project in 1939 to provide space for recreational exercise on the land and in the water. Standing on the shore, the main building is, as a report proudly described it, "streamlined and modern to the last degree," hosting sleek sculptures and stylized murals with nautical themes.[3]

If you situate yourself just right, you might be able to make out Coit Tower from Hunters Point; at this angle the tower may appear near the TransAmerica Building in the skyline. Completed in 1933, Coit Tower features interior frescoes that were a Public Works of Art Project supervised by Victor Arnautoff, who oversaw a team of some two dozen artists. The murals show a series of California scenes, both agricultural and industrial, demonstrating the power and resilience of ordinary Americans suffering the

Depression. Like Arnautoff's murals for George Washington High School (out of view from here, but to the northwest and nearer the ocean), the Coit Tower murals express both patriotism and sometimes-sharp criticism of the nation's history.

Even though you are in a neighborhood that is among the likeliest to enjoy sunshine in this frequently foggy city, you may notice the pollution in the air. People who live around here are among those in the city most likely to make an emergency room visit for asthma. On a map of the city made by California's Office of Environmental Health Hazard Assessment, seeking to identify low-income and high-pollution communities, this area appears as a red polygon—just as it did on maps made by the Home Owners Loan Corporation (HOLC) during the New Deal, whose appraisers identified areas at high risk of defaulting on a mortgage as class D, or fourth grade, and colored those regions in red. These areas tended to reflect, as the federal appraisers' guide said, the presence of "racial groups . . . which tend to lower the levels of land values." Often, as here in Hunters Point, those racial groups were black. The red lines New Deal officials drew on maps in the 1930s warned lenders away, made it harder to borrow money to buy houses here, and helped keep these neighborhoods poor and their residents politically powerless, vulnerable to the undesirable by-products of industry, beset by the construction of highways, breathing bright but dirty air. These facts of health and demography are a legacy of the New Deal too, and another reason it matters today, to a population of voters nevertheless much more likely to support it than others who benefited more generously from its policies. Perhaps no group of Americans had, or has, a more complicated relationship to the New Deal than African Americans.[4]

From the end of the Civil War onward, black Americans tended to vote Republican, casting their ballots for the party of Lincoln and emancipation, of civil rights and voting rights, the party that stamped out the first Ku Klux Klan under President Ulysses S. Grant. Sometime in the late nineteenth century, the Grand Old Party stopped regarding the rights and liberties of African Americans as a high priority, and although it is difficult to pinpoint a single date for this shift in its approach to government, there are certainly obvious landmarks along the way. Immediately after the Civil War, the U.S. Army was the agency most dependably devoted to enforcing the nation's earliest federal civil rights laws, but by the early 1870s the army had all but left the South.[5] Old Confederates returned to their prewar business in statehouses and countinghouses across the South, and legislatures dominated by Democrats began to strip the ballot from citizens who could not pass appropriate tests of literacy or wealth—mainly citizens who were black. The black politicians who had held federal office lost their seats. In 1890 the Republicans, holding the presidency and both houses of Congress, nevertheless failed to pass a voting rights bill. By the end of the decade, William McKinley, a Republican president who had fought against the rebels at Antietam, was actively seeking white southern votes, and in a speech at Atlanta he declared the federal government had a responsibility—out of what he called "a spirit of fraternity" with white southerners—to tend and honor the graves of the Confederate dead.[6] Partly in reaction to this defection, some African

Americans began to consider whether they might belong in the Democratic Party, which had begun to recast itself as the party of the American poor. As one black activist who joined the Democrats in the 1890s argued, it was time African Americans should "no longer blindly follow the Republican Party." The Democrats had become the party of the working class, those who "have made this country and we can make it over again, if we want to."[7]

Such rebels remained an exception among black voters, most of whom stayed with the Republican Party into the twentieth century. Over the course of Theodore Roosevelt's time in office, thousands of African Americans gave the president's surname as a first name to their children; despite the progressive's candid racism, he did at least venture to invite Booker T. Washington to dine at the White House, in a gesture that offended segregationists. But many black people believed Roosevelt's successor, William Howard Taft, did even less than that symbolic little, especially because Taft deferred to white southerners rather than appoint black candidates to federal posts in the South. In 1912 some civil rights leaders, including W. E. B. Du Bois, endorsed the Democratic candidate, Woodrow Wilson, as the lesser of electable evils. When Wilson went on to institute Jim Crow in the federal government, Du Bois disgustedly denounced him as "one of the most grievous disappointments that a disappointed people must bear."[8]

Republicans of the 1920s continued to cultivate white southerners. Although Warren Harding and Calvin Coolidge said they opposed lynching and supported civil rights commissions, the federal government did not pass an anti-lynching bill or seriously undertake to support civil rights. Meanwhile, Herbert Hoover, as secretary of commerce and flood-relief administrator in 1927, did much to alienate African Americans. Although white Americans in the swollen Mississippi River's path regarded Hoover as a kind of savior to the flood-inundated valley that year, black Americans felt themselves treated as second-class citizens or worse, kept in camps as workers whose labor remained essential to the region.[9]

When Hoover was the Republican nominee for president in 1928, the Democrats put forward Al Smith, a Catholic viciously opposed by the Ku Klux Klan. Sensing potential, the Smith campaign sought out Walter White, the assistant executive secretary of the NAACP, and tried to get him to manage a pro-Smith campaign among African Americans. White was tempted; after all, he believed that Hoover and his fellow Republicans had "quite obviously made up their minds to throw the Negro overboard in their efforts to Republicanize the South." But if White was ready to abandon the Republicans, the Democrats were not prepared to embrace civil rights. Smith declined to make a statement prepared by NAACP officials saying that he "would not be ruled by the anti-Negro South." White did not join the Smith campaign. The black newspaper publisher Robert Vann had a similar experience, believing that "it is no secret that Lily White Republicans and Democratic bolters in the South have formed an alliance with the hope of carrying Dixie for Hoover by completely eliminating the Negro," but when he approached Democratic Party leaders, he found them unreceptive. Although some black voters did vote for Smith in 1928, the political map was more striking for the shift of white southerners to Hoover, who won five of the eleven former

Confederate states—Virginia, North Carolina, Tennessee, Texas, and Florida.[10] As Walter White wrote, "We are going to have an entirely new political alignment—the Republicans will absorb the anti-Negro South, and become, through the compromises necessary to gain that end, the relatively anti-Negro party, while the Negro will find refuge in the Democratic Party."[11]

In addition to having a common enemy in the Klan and other American bigots, those African Americans who did support Smith found themselves drawn to his economic policies. During his career in the New York assembly and statehouse, Smith had supported legislation for improved factory conditions and a minimum wage. He stood, as one African American newspaper said, for the idea that a decent standard of living was "the right of the humblest of the nation's citizens."[12] For these "bread and butter" reasons, as the political scientist Ralph J. Bunche called them, black voters might feel inclined to vote for Democrats even if they did not focus on the cause of civil rights.[13]

Hoover, as candidate for president, did little to win over black voters; on the contrary, he did much to drive them away. His campaign refused to seat racially integrated delegations at the 1928 convention, preferring instead "lily-white" groups. The Hoover faction also blocked a proposal made by black delegates to commit the party to its traditional stance of civil rights and voting rights. The *Chicago Defender,* a leading African American newspaper, endorsed a Democratic candidate for president for the first time in its history, writing, "Our readers are entitled to know that the Ku Klux Klan is taking an active part in [this] campaign and that it is NOT aiding the Democratic candidate."[14]

Once in the White House, Hoover did even more to prove to black Americans that he had little interest in their votes, most notably by trying to put a white southern Republican with a record of opposition to civil rights on the U.S. Supreme Court. In 1930 Hoover nominated John J. Parker, a young North Carolinian, for a justiceship. Parker belonged to the new generation of Republicans who rejected the civil rights promoted by their forebears. He approved of black disfranchisement. "The participation of the Negro in politics is a source of evil and danger to both races," he declared. The NAACP campaigned against his nomination, which narrowly failed.[15]

In 1932, the American Federation of Labor (AFL) published a report finding that the treatment of black laborers on federally funded public works in the Mississippi valley resembled a "reign of terror." The union's investigation found that "government money appropriated to stimulate business and employment has been used with reverse results and to fatten the pockets of certain unscrupulous and racketeering contractors." The private firms that were meant to be relieving unemployment by hiring American laborers were paying low wages, imposing working days of twelve hours and more, requiring seven-day working weeks, beating laborers, and letting malaria spread throughout worksites. The authors concluded that African Americans were "held in virtual slavery by . . . these desecrators of the Sabbath, these floggers of men and women, these thieves of their employees' paltry wages."[16] The NAACP found likewise, publishing the results of its own investigation under the title "Mississippi River Slavery—1932." The field researcher found that by contracting the work out to private firms, the federal government had surrendered control of the worksites and permitted abuses. Like the AFL, the NAACP described the conditions as "virtual slavery," noting that starvation drove people to accept even brutal conditions to earn money for food. "Hundreds of thousands of poor, helpless black men and women are now under this juggernaut of exploitation and brutality," the NAACP concluded, urging the federal government to prevent this abuse of its money and its citizens.[17] Herbert Hoover did not reply to the NAACP's inquiries regarding these reports.[18]

While national Republican politicians had by 1932 dropped anything more than a faint rhetorical commitment to the cause of civil rights, national Democratic politicians had not yet taken it up. Democrats felt little pressure to seek the allegiance of black voters. More than 70 percent of African Americans still lived in the states of the former Confederacy and, owing to various forms of legal disfranchisement, including the poll tax and the literacy test, coupled with the threat or reality of violence, could not vote.[19] To speak out on behalf of civil rights meant alienating the voters of the South—the whites who maintained segregation and disfranchisement, and kept the region a one-party state for the Democratic Party, which limited its decisive primary elections to white voters. Challenging this structure meant, in all likelihood, losing primary elections and Electoral College votes—hence Smith's unwillingness to accept the support of Vann and White, and Roosevelt's similar unwillingness in 1932 to make civil rights explicitly a part of the New Deal.[20]

In July 1932, when Roosevelt accepted the nomination of the Democratic National Convention in person at Chicago, he pledged himself to a New Deal and foreshadowed much of what he would elaborate further in the summer and fall of the campaign: policies to relieve farmers by raising commodity prices, federal leadership in providing public works for employment, a plan of environmental rescue; overall, he offered the promise of "work, with all the moral and spiritual values that go with it; and with work, a reasonable measure of security." Underlying all his proposed policies was a moral principle: support for "the great mass of people" rather than a favored few. He promised "reconstruction" of the nation and used language familiar to Americans from the Gettysburg Address, urging, "Let us now and here highly resolve to resume the country's interrupted march along the path of real progress, of real justice, of real equality for all of our citizens, great and small." In addressing the convention himself, he had broken precedent: nominees had previously accepted their party's vote from afar. His notes for the speech included the theme "There is no room in this country for two conservative parties" and in consequence the thought "I would rather break a precedent than a promise."[21]

The easiest way to avoid breaking promises is, of course, to avoid making unkeepable commitments. So when NAACP president Joel Spingarn wrote, in response to Roosevelt's Lincolnian rhetoric and promise to march toward real equality for all citizens, a proposed speech for Roosevelt to give that would link civil rights to the New Deal, Roosevelt declined. Spingarn (who was white) conferred with the people he called his "colored advisors" to come up with something a Democratic candidate for president might say. In a supporting memorandum he observed,

"The American Negro is no longer tied hand and foot to the Republican Party." A Democrat might, with small effort, win some part of the African American vote, which "forms the balance of power in from eight to twelve northern states." Spingarn proposed therefore that Roosevelt stage a meeting with black leaders and read them something like the draft remarks Spingarn sent.

Spingarn's statement exhibited a careful blandness. "There are many races in America . . . all of them should live together without friction," it began. It continued, "The Negro should not only be given a chance to earn a living, but should be granted every opportunity to develop himself." It included an expression of "abhorrence of the crime of lynching." It proposed that black Americans receive "fair play" and their "share" of government expenditures; it did not challenge segregation. As Spingarn wrote in his covering note, "The enclosed statement would be of great service in winning the confidence of Negro voters, but is of such a nature that (with the possible exception of a single phrase) it would not alienate the white South." The sole potentially offending phrase read, "He should vote on the same terms as others vote." Spingarn mentioned that he had not written that assertion, but had added it at the request of his "colored advisors"—he set it off in handwritten red brackets to invite its deletion.[22]

Still, even so mild an expression of solidarity with black voters struck Roosevelt as an unwarranted risk. "Just between you and me," he wrote, "as a matter of pure political expediency, the less I say about this subject, the better." Wanting to hold the white southerners whom Al Smith had lost, he would not personally make a statement in support of his black constituents.[23]

But if Roosevelt was unwilling to mention civil rights himself, he was happy to have his surrogates seek black voters for the New Deal. Just a few weeks after turning down Spingarn's suggestion, Roosevelt eagerly received a report from two of his campaign officials who told him they had been looking at polling data and found that surveys of the "recently developed . . . heavy concentration of immigrant negroes from the South" in some northern and western cities showed a potential "gold mine" of support for Roosevelt. Black voters, despite their traditional allegiance to the Republican Party, liked the message of the New Deal Democrats. The campaign would simply have to ensure that these ideas got out. Roosevelt told his staffers he thought this proposal "a grand idea" and urged them to "push it vigorously." Accordingly, the campaign added a black labor leader to its roster of traveling speakers, tasked with delivering the message "The Negro is more affected by the depression than any other group . . . and it is high time that he were getting a new deal. . . . By the election of Franklin D. Roosevelt the working people will get a square deal and . . . the Negro will share in the benefits." There would be no statement by the candidate for, or specifically to, black voters, nor would the campaign offer support for civil rights—but the Democrats would extend to black voters the possibility of class solidarity.[24]

By the time of the 1932 election, the Republicans had shifted away from black voters while the Democrats had shifted toward them without embracing the cause of civil rights fully. African American editorial opinion reflected this noncommittal condition. The *Chicago Defender,* without saying anything positive about Hoover, argued that black Americans should continue voting against the Democratic Party, which was "under control of men who do not regard the rights of black people as an essential part in the interpretation of the laws of the land."[25] Somewhat further along the spectrum in recognizing the changes that had occurred in the partisan alignment, the *Atlanta Daily World* declared it could not support or oppose either candidate. "We believe the Negro may as conscientiously vote the Democratic ticket as he can the Republican, and there the matter rests."[26] And still further along in a Democratic direction, the *Pittsburgh Courier* took the view that "Roosevelt . . . said the things that every thoughtful, freedom-loving Negro wanted to hear . . . that if [he is] elected President every citizen will be treated with equal fairness, regardless of race. . . . That is all we have ever wanted."[27]

Black votes in 1932 reflected this wide range of opinion. Roosevelt did not persuade a majority of African Americans to cast their ballots for him, but he did win significant numbers—or Hoover lost them. Overall, black voters were less likely to shift to Roosevelt than other habitually Republican constituencies, but in many cities they did shift. The NAACP, analyzing the vote, concluded there had been a "National Negro Democratic Swing," such that although Roosevelt had not won over a majority of African Americans, he had done well, and in some cases better than Al Smith four years before. In New York City, he probably did get the votes of more than half the black population.[28] His first term would prove whether he could earn the right to African Americans' support.

Many agencies of the New Deal made no special effort to include African Americans and some went out of their way to exclude them, especially where white southerners administered the programs. The Tennessee Valley Authority, operating in the birthplace of the Klan, afforded black workers some opportunities but discriminated against them overall, as we have seen. And the TVA, like the Agricultural Adjustment Administration, operated by giving relief to farm owners while doing little or nothing for their tenants and employees—among whom black people were overrepresented. Officials of the National Recovery Administration, which did include some protections for laborers, eventually interpreted its jurisdiction to cover only industry, excluding agriculture—and therefore most black workers in the South, as well as Mexican American workers in the West. Where the NRA did raise wages, in industry, employers seeking to keep their costs down were likely to respond by laying off black workers. Roosevelt himself declared he had no "purpose . . . by sudden or exclusive change, to impair southern industry by refusing to recognize traditional differentials."[29] The Social Security Act of 1935 excluded domestic and agricultural workers from its old-age benefits, thus rendering a majority of black laborers ineligible. This exclusion had at least as much to do with the bureaucratic difficulty of collecting data and contributions from such jobs as it did with race. Other countries without the American history of race-based enslavement had, when enacting old-age pensions, likewise excluded these classes of workers at first. But black Americans' overrepresentation in these underpaid jobs reflected a pervasive, systemic racism that the New Deal did little to relieve.[30]

Southern Democrats in Congress played an essential role in the first phase of the New Deal. Joseph Robinson of Arkansas led the Roosevelt forces in the Senate until his sudden death during the failed effort to enlarge the federal judiciary in 1937. Hugo Black of Alabama did essential work to create the NRA and other New Deal measures. Roosevelt's vice president, the onetime Speaker of the House, John Nance Garner of Texas, served as a critical conduit to Capitol Hill for the administration. Throughout the South, white politicians who had spent their careers making use of the slogan "states' rights" suddenly found themselves willing to ignore it if doing so meant massive federal investment in hydroelectricity, roads, flood control, public health, and other benefits for their constituents.[31]

Roosevelt therefore deferred to the southern delegation's insistence on preserving white supremacy. Although Walter White identified a federal anti-lynching bill as the NAACP's chief priority in 1933, Roosevelt never fully supported it, repeatedly saying that if he did, he would lose votes he needed to get New Deal legislation through. He did denounce lynching as "vile," saying that modern Americans could not rest "content with preaching against" it, and cautiously recommended some kind of nonspecific government action.[32] White launched a publicity campaign around the nation and got backing for the bill in Congress, including the sectionally diverse sponsorship of senators Edward Costigan of Virginia and Robert Wagner of New York. Their proposal would allow federal prosecutions of lynchings if local jurisdictions failed to bring a case; the penalty might include a substantial fine of the county where the lynching occurred. Asked about this bill in 1934, Roosevelt said he was certainly opposed to lynching and wanted to see something done but was unsure that he would favor that bill. "I am absolutely for the objective. . . . I told them to go ahead and try to get a vote on it."[33] With such lukewarm presidential support behind the effort, Robinson knew he could without penalty prevent the Costigan-Wagner bill from getting a hearing in the Senate. Other anti-lynching bills met similar fates, even though public opinion was broadly in favor of such legislation. The southern filibuster in the Senate proved too strong. If a bill passed the House, it never reached a vote in the Senate because the South stood solidly against it. Nor were southern senators subtle about the reasons for their stand. "I believe in white supremacy," Allen Ellender of Louisiana said, "and as long as I am in the Senate I expect to fight for white supremacy."[34] By then it was 1938. As before, Roosevelt began to say that he could not afford to press for anti-lynching legislation when relief of the unemployed remained his greatest priority: he needed Congress to pass a new emergency relief appropriation to counteract the recession that had set in the year before. Still, he told his son Jimmy to talk to James Byrnes, senator from South Carolina, to see what might be done. Jimmy Roosevelt telephoned Byrnes and said, "Father would like to know what likelihood there is of the filibuster's ending." Byrnes replied, "Tell him not until the year 2038, unless the bill is withdrawn before then!"[35]

Beyond the South, New Deal programs sometimes left existing segregation untouched and even expanded it into new areas, perpetuating it for new generations. Most notably, housing programs that gave the benefits of homeownership to millions of Americans tended to leave black people out. When white southerners implemented New Deal programs, they reproduced Jim Crow; when real estate professionals implemented New

Deal programs, they produced a new and subtler form of racial exclusion.

The Depression created a crisis of loan default and foreclosure, as homeowners suffering from the economic downturn could not meet their payments. It also entailed a crisis in the housing industry; with few people able to buy houses, there was little profit to be made in building them. The New Deal tried to address both these problems. Most notably, the Home Owners' Loan Corporation of 1933 sought to buy and refinance, on favorable terms, underwater mortgages. Together with the Federal National Mortgage Association (FNMA, better known as Fannie Mae) of 1938, which created an investment market for mortgages, the HOLC put the federal government in the business of helping lenders to determine the interest, term, down-payment requirements, and other basic elements of financing a house purchase. Equally important, the Federal Housing Administration (FHA) of 1934 insured lenders making loans for housing repairs and purchases, which put the federal government into a partnership with firms assessing whether or not a prospective borrower qualified as an acceptable risk. When creating these agencies, Congress generally did not determine the details of eligibility, but left them up to the bureaucrats and bankers and other businesspeople who would make, buy, sell, and insure loans.[36]

When deciding what a house might be worth, the HOLC and FHA worked with real estate agents and credit-reporting firms to determine the quality of neighborhoods and borrowers. They considered how big the average lot was, how far the houses were set back from the street, and how much money the borrower could put down. These considerations favored newer, suburban construction and homeowners who already had money. New suburbs often had racially exclusive covenants, and black people were less likely to have accumulated the 20 or 30 percent of a purchase price than white people. The rules for evaluating a house or borrower therefore contained implicit biases even when they did not expressly mention race—although they sometimes did that, too. The FHA's instructions for evaluating risk when underwriting included an injunction to consider the presence of "racial groups" that might lower values. Consensus opinion among experts, social scientists, lenders, and real estate brokers supported segregation: "If a neighborhood is to retain stability it is necessary that properties shall continue to be occupied by the same social and racial classes."[37]

Although the New Deal is often rightly regarded as giving Americans a closer relation with the federal government—and indeed, that was one of Roosevelt's major intentions—it also extended new power to the states and local governments, and to private enterprise as well. The housing programs, as well as the TVA and some of the New Deal construction programs, invested these agencies with new authority. They had to; they operated within a series of constraints, not least of which was the insistent sense of emergency: people were starving and whatever must be done, must be done quickly. It was quicker to rely on existing experts and practitioners than to train new ones. And by definition, giving more power to the institutions and people who already held it lent strength to conservatism of all kinds, including in the matter of race.[38]

Yet despite this ineffectuality, ambivalence, and harm, black voters came more and more to support Roosevelt and the New Deal. The number of black children given the name "Roosevelt" swelled into the thousands, as it had during Theodore's presidency. And in 1936, even though Republicans tried to win black voters' support once more, African Americans contributed to the president's record-breaking landslide reelection. Whereas Roosevelt had won a bare majority of black voters in New York City in 1932, now he won more than 80 percent there—and 75 percent in Pittsburgh, 66 percent in Detroit, and majorities or large pluralities elsewhere. In 1932, black Americans had lagged behind other constituencies in shifting to the New Deal; in 1936, they more than caught up with their fellow countrymen.[39]

The reasons were not far to seek. If the New Deal's efforts to assist black Americans were halting and small and always coupled with some slight or setback, they nevertheless existed. The historian Rayford Logan, who both advised and criticized the administration, remarked, "Treating Negroes as human beings was a very significant factor" in earning their support.[40] The inequitably distributed benefits of the New Deal nevertheless did, as the Roosevelt campaign had promised in 1932, go principally to poor and needy people, among whom black Americans were numerous. For some African American voters, then, the decision to support Roosevelt for reelection was simple: they didn't "think it is fair, to eat Roosevelt bread and meat and vote for Gov. Landon." Just as poorer Americans generally were more likely to support Roosevelt, so too were poorer African Americans.[41]

The New Deal's treatment of black Americans as human beings went beyond the delivery of benefits to consulting black advisors for their expert views. At first, the Roosevelt administration pursued what looked like an unpromising approach. In August 1933, it established an Office of the Special Adviser on the Economic Status of Negroes and promptly hired a white southerner, Clark Foreman, to run it, producing consternation among black Americans. But Foreman wanted to prove he was serious about his charge, and within a few months hired the young black economist Robert Weaver, who had produced studies critical of the New Deal's effects on black employment. Another white southerner in the administration, Secretary of Commerce Daniel Roper, hired the executive secretary of the Urban League, Eugene Kinckle Jones, as an advisor on the problems faced by black-owned businesses. Even if these appointments were meant in part for show, they put ambitious African Americans in positions to influence policy and appointments. Weaver had come to the attention of New Dealers by using statistical disparities to demonstrate a pattern of discrimination in hiring on public works and, in office, he managed to get the PWA to adopt policies for countering such discrimination. By 1936 he could write with satisfaction that the policy of acting to counter "prima facie discrimination has proven to be a successful means of protecting Negro labor on Federal projects." In addition, Weaver secured the appointment of his friend the lawyer William Hastie as the investigator in charge of enforcing nondiscrimination policies.[42]

Weaver and Hastie forced immediate basic changes in the administration. They insisted on being seated and served in the Department of the Interior's segregated dining room. White cafeteria workers reported them to Ickes and asked him what he was going to do about it. "Not a damned thing, ladies," he said, and afterward issued an order ending Jim Crow in the department.[43]

Their influence extended further yet; increasingly, senior administration officials listened to them, if not always or even adequately. In December 1933, black appointees and sympathetic white ones, including Foreman, attended the first meeting of a self-constituted group of advisors to discuss the treatment of African Americans in New Deal programs. Shortly afterward, Ickes met Roosevelt to suggest that the group be made an official body. The president refused, but he charged Ickes with attempting to ensure that all departments and major New Deal programs had at least one advisor devoted to the study of black Americans' concerns, and asked Ickes to convene them periodically for discussion. There would be no formal committee of black advisors—that would be too upsetting to white southerners—but there would be a periodic meeting of black advisors.[44] By March, Eugene Davidson, a columnist for the Associated Negro Press, was referring to the group as "the black cabinet," a name that stuck. Describing the New Deal as a bloodless "revolution" and the president as "a radical," Davidson believed the black advisors would ensure a place for black Americans in the progress being made.[45]

Over time, an increasing number of black people held jobs in the administration, at senior and lower levels alike. More black people had relief work. The PWA turned its attention to building new schools for African Americans in the South—one of the first items cut by local governments in the Depression—which, according to one historian, "rescued black education in the South."[46] Black workers even, increasingly, had skilled work in New Deal construction programs.[47]

The formation in 1935 of the Works Progress Administration, a federally administered jobs program under Harry Hopkins with a nondiscrimination policy of its own, boded well for African American participation in the New Deal. So did the appointment of Mary McLeod Bethune, a nationally known civil rights activist, to a position of importance in Hopkins's offices.[48] And from outside the administration in the same year, the formation of the Committee for Industrial Organization (CIO) within the American Federation of Labor began an era of labor organization that sought to include black workers.

The CIO's commitment to recruiting black workers attracted support from civil rights organizations across the political spectrum, ranging from communist-influenced groups on the left to the more mainstream NAACP, whose *Crisis* magazine editorialized in the fall of 1936 that racial discrimination in the AFL was "not to be denied," and declared that with the new CIO's principles, "black workers ought to flock to the CIO unhesitatingly."[49] The CIO's promotion of race-blind class interests, coupled with African Americans' generally pro-labor stance, made the new labor organization the most effective advocate of civil rights among institutions not specifically devoted to that purpose. And with the boost to unionization generated by the National Labor Relations Act, or Wagner Act, of 1935, the New Deal and labor depended increasingly on each other.[50]

The more the New Deal became associated with the cause of labor unions and civil rights, the more conservatives, and particularly white southerners, began to look with suspicion on the programs of the Roosevelt administration. The Ku Klux Klan abhorred the CIO, which, as the Klan's *Fiery Cross* declared in a headline, "wants whites and blacks on [the] same level."[51] In this matter, southern chambers of commerce had the same concerns as the Klan, having long supported low wages in the region. Even though the CIO's threat in the South was more symbolic than real—it made little progress in southern towns where black citizens were barred from voting—the specter of racial integration and industrial unionism provided a powerful incentive for conservatives to push back.[52] Conservative southern Democrats made common cause with Republicans in the Congress, increasingly standing against New Deal measures in Roosevelt's second term.[53]

In response, the president targeted conservative Democrats in the 1938 primaries, including southerners Walter George of Georgia, Ellison "Cotton Ed" Smith of South Carolina, and Millard Tydings of Maryland. At his second home in Georgia, Roosevelt said all the people of the South needed the benefits of a liberal program of legislation, urging voters to "send . . . Senators and Representatives who are willing to stand up and fight night and day for . . . laws with teeth in them which go to the root of the problems, which remove the inequities."[54] This "purge," as critical journalists and politicians called it, largely failed in the near term; almost all the conservative incumbents retained their seats despite presidential opposition. But it succeeded in distinguishing the New Deal from the traditional Democratic Party and in defining Rooseveltian liberalism as something new, focused on accepting the new racial composition of the Democratic electorate.[55]

If the primaries of 1938 were a disappointment for liberals, the general elections brought a further setback. The Democrats lost substantial numbers of seats in both houses of Congress, although they retained their majorities. Republican gains in northern districts displaced liberals. As a result, conservatives dominated the Democratic congressional delegations; the House Democratic caucus was majority southern. Moreover, the Munich crisis and then Kristallnacht brought the Nazi threat to the forefront of politics in the United States as elsewhere, shifting focus away from domestic concerns to foreign policy. Roosevelt could have decided likewise to shift away from the New Deal and his efforts to remake the Democratic Party into a liberal party.

One of the liberals who lost office in the 1938 election was Frank Murphy, governor of Michigan, who, fearing that the president would do just that, wrote to urge him otherwise. The New Deal needed strengthening and expanding, with more people included in its jobs programs and its social security provisions. "The signs of the times here and abroad suggest to me," Murphy wrote, that "our democratic institutions" remained under threat, as they had in 1933.[56]

Roosevelt was probably not so much swayed by Murphy's case for doubling down on the New Deal's liberalism as impressed by the resolve of a kindred spirit. And he had need in his administration of someone attuned to the Nazi threat. The retirement of Attorney General Homer Cummings left an opening at the top of the Department of Justice, and Murphy filled it in January 1939. Scarcely had Murphy taken office when he received a letter from the CIO's chief counsel and president urging him to consider that Reconstruction-era civil rights legislation could be used to protect unions from losing rights guaranteed them by federal statute—in this case, the right to organize, as guaranteed by the National Labor Relations Act. Murphy, a longtime supporter of civil rights for African Americans and a member of the NAACP, took this notion and expanded it into a brief for civil rights more generally.[57]

On February 3, Murphy issued an order establishing the Civil Liberties Unit in the Department of Justice, consisting of seven attorneys, "to make a study of the provisions of the Constitution of the United States and the Acts of Congress relating to civil rights with reference to present conditions . . . and to direct, supervise and conduct prosecutions." The announcement garnered attention from African American newspapers eager to see the Department of Justice do what, in 1870, it had been created to do: enforce civil rights law.[58]

Murphy accepted Roosevelt's nomination to the Supreme Court before the Civil Liberties Unit completed its survey of available civil rights legislation, so it was his replacement as attorney general, Robert Jackson, who oversaw the implementation of Murphy's civil rights initiative, with a memorandum outlining its jurisdiction issued May 21, 1940. The unit—now renamed the Civil Liberties Section, and soon to be renamed again as the Civil Rights Section—agreed with the CIO that federal law could be used to protect unions, and also prevent lynchings, and forestall "deprivation of negro voting rights at Federal elections." Specifically, they believed they could, and should, bring a case to the Supreme Court to establish "Federal interest in a primary" election. If they could get a favorable decision in that matter, then federal civil rights law would apply to the Democratic primaries in the South, making it unlawful to restrict those critical elections only to white voters.[59]

Within weeks, the question of where the New Deal stood on civil rights came to Roosevelt publicly, and rather against the president's will. At a gathering of the communist-influenced American Youth Congress, Roosevelt received repeated questions about his stand on lynching, the poll tax, and violent disfranchisement. He demurred, saying, "There is a time element. You cannot get it in one year or two. We are all working and in time it will happen." He alluded to the Senate filibuster: "If you can get a vote on the Antilynching Bill in the Senate it would go through—we all know it." He could point to only one hope: as the Civil Rights Section had just explained, the Supreme Court might be pressed to rule in favor of black civil rights. Posing the rhetorical question, "What about the court ruling, the Supreme Court?" he allowed, "That is a possibility."[60]

It was a possibility that would, within a few weeks more, become a likelihood. The Louisiana primary that year included, not unusually, a case of blatant fraud. Election officials, including one named Patrick Classic, had simply erased vote counts and written in ones they found preferable. They had thus deprived voters of their rights—not, specifically, black voters; but to establish the narrow precedent that the federal government had an interest in the integrity of primary elections, race did not have to be a factor in the case. The civil rights attorneys of the Justice Department brought the case, knowing they would lose it based on existing law. But Justice Department officials ensured that the district judge write a clear opinion that would allow them to appeal and challenge precedent in higher courts. Thus sped through the lower jurisdiction, the case arrived in the Supreme Court early in 1941 as *United States v. Classic.* The civil rights lawyers argued that because "as a matter of unbroken practice, the Democratic primary election determines the victor at the general election," the primary was "not only an integral part of the process; it is the determinative part" of the election. Therefore federal election law, to have any effect, must apply to the primary.[61]

The Court agreed. The primary was clearly the election in Louisiana, as in other parts of the South, and therefore to take away the right to vote in a primary, or conspire to do so, constituted a violation of federal civil rights law.[62] When the opinion became public, black newspapers and activists understood its clear implication almost immediately: discrimination on the basis of race in a primary must therefore be unlawful. To establish this point explicitly, William Hastie and Thurgood Marshall brought a new case to the Supreme Court, *Smith v. Allwright,* under the auspices of the NAACP Legal Defense and Education Fund (LDF), challenging the all-white primary in Texas. The Department of Justice decided not to join this new case for political reasons. "We have already assisted the negroes by winning the *Classic* case which gives them their principal ammunition," wrote an attorney in an internal memorandum. "Should we go further in their behalf and make a gesture which cannot fail to offend many others, in Texas and the South generally, in a case in which we are not a party? I think not."[63] And the *Classic* case did indeed provide the principal reasoning on which *Smith v. Allwright* depended; the NAACP LDF brief's first reason for overturning the white primary began, "The Constitution and laws of the United States as construed in United States v. Classic prohibit interference by respondents with petitioner's right to vote in Texas Democratic primaries."[64]

In fostering voting rights for African Americans in the South while eschewing any public claim to credit—or blame—for doing it, the Roosevelt Justice Department was continuing the equivocal and ambivalent tradition of the New Deal. Black voters' assessments of the choices available to them led them to support the Democrats. Beholden though it remained to the vicious segregationists of its southern wing, the national party had come to represent workers' rights, voting rights, and civil rights. And it remained the most powerful political institution throughout the South. As the political scientist Ralph Bunche wrote in 1940, NAACP branches in the South tended to support and lobby Democrats because theirs was "the *only* party." Bunche regarded class-consciousness as the best hope for African Americans, writing, "If there is any ideology which offers any hope to the Negro it would seem to me that which identifies his interests with the white workers of the nation."[65]

Even with material interests in common, black and white Americans could take different views of the same event. For example, Bunche noted, segregation ensured that black people had limited choices. It was possible that the only movie theater in a black neighborhood might offer, as its sole screening, the 1939 hit *Gone with the Wind.* Would-be African American filmgoers could either skip the cinema or sit in a Jim Crow theater while watching a movie about the tragic grandeur of white slavers. "Some Negroes might wish to go, however," Bunche wrote, "even under these conditions, just to see the Yankees burn Atlanta."[66] Americans might, together, endure the Great Depression, work for the WPA, fight a world war—but white and black people could rightly derive different lessons from the experiences.

Likewise, white southerners could see in the New Deal a program that brought the benefits of better roads, irrigation, and electrical power to their region, while black southerners could see in it a program that gave them better jobs, better working conditions, and the chance to vote. The Roosevelt administration was able to maintain a political equilibrium that was possible only in that moment, keeping the loyalty of white southerners while eroding their absolute hold on political power. A few decades later it would not be possible for a Democratic president to avoid choosing one above the other.

Outside the South, black Americans gained and lost in subtler, but still consequential, ways. In the North and the West, African Americans could vote and gain work and still suffer from discrimination. Black voters retained an extraordinary, and personally unearned, sense of loyalty to Franklin Roosevelt to the end of the president's life, regarding him—as many poorer white Americans did—as more than a desirable politician, something akin to a friend. On April 28, 1945, the former boxer and blues pianist "Champion" Jack Dupree released "F.D.R. Blues," opining that "FDR . . . helped everybody, right unto the end" and declaring that the old Knickerbocker was a "credit to our race." Roosevelt largely escaped critical assessment for the long-term effects of continuing discrimination.[67]

Occasionally, modern politicians see both New Deals. Congresswoman Alexandria Ocasio-Cortez has urged her constituents to remember the discriminatory housing policies of the New Deal, noting that they "accelerated many parts of an already horrific racial wealth gap." Yet Ocasio-Cortez also uses the language and imagery of the other New Deal, the occasion for "national, social, industrial, and economic mobilization" in the belief that in the twenty-first century, a "Green New Deal" could re-create "the greatest middle class the United States has ever seen," while ensuring the inclusion of "frontline and vulnerable communities." It would mean reviving the energy and ambition that rebuilt the San Francisco peninsula during the New Deal, while ensuring that the advantages of such projects accrued equitably to communities like the one at Hunters Point.[68]

5 the street where you live

A walk around your neighborhood and an investigation of public works programs, the idea of economic security, and the country the New Deal helped to build

In earlier chapters, I've asked you to consider a specific and sometimes spectacular location modified or created by the New Deal. We have seen how the New Deal wrought immense changes in the political and literal landscape, often through awe-inspiring projects. And certainly we could continue a tour of the New Deal by looking at airports and bridges and dams. But in this chapter, instead of taking you to a landmark location, I want you to consider the New Deal's impact through its more modest, but not therefore less consequential, efforts that affect nearly everybody, and begin, as the chapter title suggests, in your neighborhood.

During the spring of 2020, states and counties throughout the United States, like governments throughout the world, issued shelter-in-place orders to control the spread of the novel coronavirus. In the interest of public health, governors, county supervisors, city councils, and other authorities instructed people to remain home except for essential trips outside. But even under those orders, you could generally still go out for exercise, so long as you kept yourself a safe distance from other people and wore a mask to keep water vapor from your breath away from strangers. For many Americans, deprived of access to their gyms and swimming pools and court sports, a good brisk walk was the best way to get their hearts and lungs working. And with the reduced traffic—most people had no essential need to drive a car frequently—the air was often fresher, the sky bluer, and the soundscape freer of the hum of machines than at any time anyone could remember. A walk, even down the street where you live, could become a luxury and a voyage into unfamiliar territory. If you took advantage of this time to get out and get around, you might well have spent time on one of the more commonplace legacies of the New Deal: sidewalks.

Throughout the United States, innumerable rectangles of pavement remain that were first poured by laborers employed by the Works Progress Administration (later the name changed to the Work Projects Administration but the abbreviation WPA remained the same). These sidewalks bear a stamp of the agency's initials and, generally, the year they were created; the WPA sidewalk nearest me says it dates from 1938. Begun in 1935, the WPA lasted until 1943, when war work wiped out the need for it. Over the course of its existence, WPA workers laid about twenty-four thousand miles of new sidewalks and improved another seven thousand more.[1] These strips of concrete were, and remain, valuable beautification measures for a neighborhood. They also provide safety: as one report reflecting on the value of the new pavements dryly put it, "Juxtaposition of children and elderly adults to moving automobiles is an undesirable state of affairs."[2]

Or perhaps, if you went outdoors in that pandemic spring, you noticed that vehicular traffic had shrunk nearly to nil, and so decided it was safe to walk in the road itself. Many people did, to keep their prescribed distance from one another, and also, honestly, for a cheap bit of novelty, the chance to see their neighborhood from a new, previously unsafe perspective. Some cities closed streets to all but essential automotive access. Oakland, California, thus created out of its asphalt grid ordinarily restricted to automobiles seventy-four miles of suddenly safer walkways, wider than sidewalks and usable for exercise and recreation. Other cities—Boston, Minneapolis, and Portland, Oregon, among them—did the same.[3] Some of those roads, like the nation's sidewalks, were built or improved by New Deal workers in the 1930s. Highways, roads, and streets accounted for the largest single part of the WPA's work. Almost 38 percent of the agency's total expenditures went into roadwork, and in the peak years of New Deal employment, almost 44 percent of its workers labored to improve the nation's roads.[4]

When offered federal funds to create jobs on public works, city and county officials' thoughts turned most speedily to roadwork. During the Depression, with so many people unemployed, local treasuries dwindled. Less tax revenue came in, more aid to the poor went out. Governments decided it was better to let thoroughfares fall into ruin than permit people to starve. So when the Roosevelt administration established jobs programs, beleaguered municipalities seized the opportunity to catch up on the upkeep they had left undone during the hard years after the crash. The WPA helped American cities resume their duties, repairing and repaving carriageways and concourses. Then, after a few years of public work, with this maintenance gap closed and economic recovery under way, some of those refinished streets began to see more traffic than they could smoothly bear. As the economy grew, Americans had places to go in their cars and goods to deliver in their trucks. Congestion set in. WPA workers brought their picks and shovels to bear on this need, too, widening streets and highways and adding roads both through and between cities. Not only was there plenty of roadwork that needed doing, it was a kind of public work well suited to the crisis of the Depression. It could begin quickly, without much in the way of architectural or engineering preliminaries, and almost any laborer could do some part of the work. During the WPA's eight years of operation, its workers put in 67,000 miles of city streets and 572,000 miles of rural roads, often adding necessary guardrails, drainage works, and even small bridges as well.[5] The network of roads constructed before World War II did much to make possible the economic growth that began after it; as one economic historian wrote, these improvements "literally helped pave the way for the postwar suburbanization boom."[6]

And if, when out for exercise in an American city, you do come across a paved rectangle with a WPA stamp on it, and then proceed to the place where the pavement debouches into the street, you will almost certainly find your way eased by a ramp descending to the asphalt surface. The ramp, while not itself built by the New Deal, is nevertheless also a part of its legacy. The social security legislation passed in 1935, although best known for its old-age pensions, included other provisions to render society more generally secure, including unemployment insurance and, for the first time, a permanent federal program of responsibility for disabled Americans.[7] In charging the Committee on Economic Security with recommending ways to provide for "the men, women, and

children of the nation," the president asked his advisors to consider how to adapt "this man-made world of ours" to all the de-
bilitating conditions in which Americans found themselves
through no fault of their own—unemployment, old age, or disability.[8] Unable to walk without difficulty or assistance, Roosevelt
had long sought a way to move Americans beyond the marginal-
ization of people with disabilities, to help create a society that
could treat people like him as full citizens with a proper place in
the American community.[9] The Social Security Act of 1935 began
a tradition of shared responsibility that extended to the Americans with Disabilities Act of 1990—and also to those sidewalk
ramps.

This commitment to a more inclusive man-made world (to
borrow Roosevelt's phrase) was the most important characteristic
of the New Deal programs for public works. Too often we look
back on them as an effort merely at economic stimulus—a way to
jolt into action an economy that had sunk into lethargy. And
certainly New Dealers thought of them as serving that purpose,
hoping to put money into the pockets of Americans most likely
to spend it and thus to increase the demand for goods and services in the U.S. economy.[10] But that was only part, and perhaps
not even the most important part, of what they hoped to achieve.
Roosevelt and his advisors wanted the public works program to
revive not only the economy but also democracy. The New Dealers hoped to spur both "social and economic recovery," as relief
administrator Harry Hopkins said. By not merely giving money
to Americans but hiring them to work on the improvement of
their own country, Roosevelt and his administration wanted to

show Americans that as they worked for the government, so the government worked for them. The roads and sidewalks—and post offices, schools, parks, playgrounds, airports, harbors, and innumerable other constructions—they provided citizens public spaces in which we are not merely welcome, but which belong to us and give us pride.[11] This intention was clearest in the jobs programs' much smaller, but profoundly important, commitment to art.

Maybe you have seen photographs or paintings of WPA workers on a road somewhere in America during the New Deal. There are many such depictions of the men—and for roadwork, they would have been men—laboring in their hard denim trousers, cut loose and practical: the kind of jeans that connoisseurs today will pay a fortune to purchase from a boutique, but which then declared unequivocally that you were a laborer. The men in the picture probably also wear soft cloth caps to protect their heads from the sun, and the sweat on their faces makes a paste with the dust thrown up by picks and chisels. They are pouring, smoothing, and painting, making streets and curbs and pavements. If you have seen a depiction of these workers at their toil, there is a good chance the artwork was itself a New Deal creation. Notably, the Federal Art Project of the WPA employed painters, printmakers, photographers, and all manner of other artists who could not be expected to punch a time clock or meet a quota, but whose work the agency nevertheless endeavored to ensure and respect. As Hopkins said when asked why artists should get public works money, "Hell! They've got to eat just like other people."[12]

Although artwork accounted for a tiny share of the WPA payroll and budget, it made an outsized contribution to the way Americans thought about the New Deal, especially when public art specifically depicted New Deal labor. A 1939 photograph, often reprinted, shows WPA workers with tools and paintbrushes working to put in a new curb on a street; near them, an artist works at an easel, sketching their portrait in charcoal.[13] The roadworkers were employed by the WPA and so was the artist, Alfred Castagne.[14] The photographer is unknown, but there is a good chance that artist too was working for the WPA. Critics sometimes objected to public funding for work like this because, as a *Washington Post* editorial argued, it "smacks of propaganda rather than art." The newspaper's editorial board contended that public art programs "should sedulously refuse to sponsor" such depictions.[15]

The artists and their employers ignored such advice. Through the federally sponsored visual arts, the New Deal not only showed Americans at all kinds of daily work, it often ennobled their most ordinary undertakings. Sometimes this art was spectacular in scale and scope; for example, the 110-foot-long, 8-foot-high WPA mural Edward Laning painted for an Ellis Island building, *The Role of the Immigrant in the Industrial Development of America.* This epic history in pictures began with immigrants' debarkation at the docks and proceeded through their various fields of endeavor, from coal mining to laying railroad tracks (the illustration of which showed immigrants of Asian as well as European backgrounds).[16] Most pieces of New Deal art were more modest, aiming to put their messages into everyday life, like the painting of grape pickers on the wall of the post office in St. Helena, California, in Napa Valley wine country, reminding the community that the vintners and viticulturists rely on workers who bend their backs in the vineyards. Large or small, such art hanging in public places showed Americans doing physical labor, dignified in their strength. It gave people a way to think of themselves as important and honored in their work, in the manner ordinarily reserved for merchants and politicians. From the beginning of the New Deal, its proponents emphasized the importance of giving gravity and dignity to labor. Indeed, it was central to Franklin Roosevelt's idea of what government was supposed to do even before he ran for the presidency. And yet it took some years, and some false starts, for New Dealers to establish an ongoing commitment to public employment, learning hard lessons from their efforts as they went—beginning with Roosevelt's time as governor of New York.

The New York state senate and assembly convened in special joint session on August 28, 1931, and greeted Governor Franklin Roosevelt with applause. Reading his message to the lawmakers, he began with a more philosophical question than politicians ordinarily consider: "What is the State?" Roosevelt wanted to return to first principles so that he could persuade legislators to undertake a novel program: direct employment of citizens to provide them relief from the Depression.[17]

The general idea that governments should use public works to employ people who had lost their jobs owing to economic recession was not new. In 1925, the American Construction Council met to propose coordination of industry and government to stabilize the demand for work from industry. The council received a letter of support from the secretary of commerce, who acknowledged "the importance of the construction industry in the minimizing of the business cycle," and supported the notion that "government and public works generally should be so planned as to be of assistance in this direction." The secretary of commerce was Herbert Hoover and the president of the American Construction Council was Franklin D. Roosevelt. Their agreement in this matter did not suggest they stood at the vanguard of policy thinking; rather, it reflected a widespread view that scheduling public works and keeping some in reserve might lessen the human toll of economic downturns. Hoover had previously endorsed this view during the Conference on Unemployment in 1921.[18]

In the 1920s, civic leaders like Hoover and Roosevelt thought in terms of an effective practical arrangement among business leaders and local politicians, not a fundamental social obligation. But the scale of the Depression provoked profounder thinking. As president, Hoover offered an articulate philosophical defense against the outcry for greater public spending. "This is not a question as to whether people shall go hungry or cold in the United States. It is a solely a question of the best method by which hunger and cold shall be prevented." Hoover argued that "voluntary giving and the responsibility of local government" were preferable to "appropriations out of the Federal Treasury," for the most basic of reasons. "My own conviction is strongly that if we break down this sense of responsibility of individual generosity to individual and mutual self-help in the country in times of national difficulty and if we start appropriations of this character we have not only impaired something infinitely valuable in the life of the American people but have struck at the roots of self-government."[19] Hoover did not altogether oppose an increase of public works. But to ensure the safety of democracy, he wanted public works to remain a small part of any relief effort, preferring to see charity and community organizations take care of the need. In the latter part of 1931, Hoover estimated with some satisfaction that seven hundred thousand American families were earning their livelihoods from federal public works. Yet at the time, more than ten times as many Americans still lacked jobs, their families needing sustenance. Despite the magnitude of this hardship, which dwarfed the federal effort to address it, Hoover argued that "the Federal government is taking its part in aid to unemployment through the advancement and enlargement of public works" and that local governments were also already "doing their full part." Any "further margin of relief" necessary "must be provided by voluntary action." For Hoover, it was a more important principle that public spending remain small enough to leave room for the private sector than that it be large enough to meet the need.[20]

At nearly the same time, Roosevelt took the opposite view: not only had the crisis grown beyond the capacity of charity and local governments to meet it, the nature of self-government required aggressive public action to meet the emergency. Addressing the assembled legislators at Albany in 1931, he argued that "modern society, acting through its Government, owes the definite obligation to prevent the starvation or the dire want of any of its fellow men and women who try to maintain themselves but cannot." People involuntarily suffering unemployment became the responsibility of the state just like the elderly or the disabled, "not as a matter of charity, but as a matter of social duty." In just two years of the great slump, he reminded his audience, individual citizens' savings and credit had been exhausted; so too had the generosity of employers and the resources of private charities. Local governments either "have approached or are approaching their constitutional debt limit or for other equally good reasons, will find themselves unable greatly to add to employment on public works." Thus, "by process of elimination," the state and federal government remained. Optimistically, Roosevelt said, "The Federal Government may take action"—but he followed up more realistically by saying, "The State of New York cannot wait for that." He therefore asked the legislature to make an extraordinary appropriation of $20 million to support the operation of a new relief agency that would be, in a twice-reassuring name, not only "emergency" but "temporary." The Temporary Emergency Relief Administration (TERA), funded by an income tax, would supply public work at the prevailing wage and on a five-day week for the jobless of New York. Mindful that many of the unemployed might not, out of pride, come forward of their own accord to seek this new form of public assistance, Roosevelt said the TERA would also employ "the women of our State" to identify the needy so they could receive offers of public work.[21]

In cases where there was no available or appropriate public work, the governor said, the TERA might provide aid in kind to make sure that New Yorkers did not go without food, shelter, warmth, or clothes—but people would not receive cash relief. The state would happily pay wages, but "under no circumstances shall any actual money be paid in the form of a dole," Roosevelt insisted. He emphasized this point privately as well as publicly. "I have tried to outline my program in such a way that the dole will be avoided," he wrote in a letter. "The important thing is to provide any kind of useful public work for the benefit of those who are now unable to find employment and to furnish the necessaries of life only when useful employment cannot be found." To Roosevelt, it was vital that the state provide its citizens with the dignity of earning a living by work, not merely hand out monetary assistance.[22]

The New York state legislature passed Roosevelt's proposal, making him the first governor to establish a public works program dedicated to fighting the Depression. He asked the businessman Jesse Straus, of Macy's department store, to set up the TERA; Straus, in turn, picked Harry Hopkins, then director of the New York Tuberculosis and Health Association, to run the new agency. Hopkins brought his experience and connections from the world of charity work to bear on the challenge of swiftly setting up a new bureaucracy. Within a short time the TERA was providing work and aid for 10 percent of the state's families. Over the course of the next six years, at one bad time or another, some 40 percent of New Yorkers had recourse to TERA assistance.[23]

Thus, long before campaigning for the presidency, Roosevelt had established publicly his commitment to an expanded conception of the state's obligations, and also yoked his idea of state-sponsored welfare to work.[24] When Roosevelt noted that some

New Yorkers would have too much pride to ask for help, he was indicating that his antipathy to direct relief was not some imposition upon the poor, but rather a reflection of Americans' own values. He reckoned that people who did not want money in the form of charity might be happy to accept it as a wage. And if the state undertook to pay that wage, Roosevelt reasoned, it would in turn demonstrate that the American form of government could still function effectively, no matter what the fascists of the world might say.

Roosevelt argued that the state's duty to provide work became necessary as democratic government evolved. As human societies increased in size and complexity, the once "intimate relation" between citizens and the state grew distant. Officers of the government tended no longer to see individual persons: "Men and women are becoming mere units in statistics. This is not human progress." The need to renew a humane spirit in public service was most pressing in the area of unemployment relief. Jobless people were at their most vulnerable to the careless slights of an indifferent state machinery. But, Roosevelt believed, if the state itself employed citizens, it stopped being some remote entity and became embodied in visible people: supervisors and coworkers. An abstract bureaucracy thus reacquired a humanly comprehensible scale. Public hiring would save more than the economy: it could save democracy.[25]

Offering employment to Americans thrown out of work became a centerpiece of Roosevelt's campaign for the presidency. When seeking votes, he gave depth and complexity to his initial pledge, upon accepting the Democratic nomination for president on July 2, 1932, of a New Deal for the American people. As presidential candidate, as he had as governor, Roosevelt argued repeatedly that a public works program constituted no mere measure for recovery—not just, as we would say in modern terms, a "stimulus" to the economy—but constituted one part of a larger program to improve the health of American democracy. All his proposals had to work together, he told Americans, just as all Americans had to work together. Throughout the campaign, he insisted repeatedly on the notion of a broadly shared recovery spurred by a wide spectrum of policies. He favored a policy of what he called "social justice," rejecting policies that favored the rich so "they will let a part of their prosperity trickle down," in favor of policies that would "make the average of mankind comfortable and secure" so "their prosperity will rise upward, just as yeast rises up."[26] Recovery could not begin anywhere unless it began everywhere: "Interdependence is the watchword of this age," he claimed, and he repeated that word through the course of his canvass.[27]

This emphasis on interdependence meant everything returned to the need for public employment. Farmers had grown to be interdependent with factories and vice versa—so too capital and labor, East and West, North and South, Americans and the peoples of other nations.[28] As president, Roosevelt pledged he would raise farm prices not just to benefit farmers, but to "restore the purchasing power of the farmer" as consumer, to spur demand for manufactured goods. Reducing the acreage devoted to farming could also improve the environment; fields once cultivated could become forest once more. Public employees could speed reforestation by planting trees and curating these new forests: "It needs the aid of man to clear out the dead wood and encourage only the growth that will best serve the national need. . . . Here again is another field for the employment of great numbers of our citizens."[29]

Public employment remained paramount, even when Roosevelt tried to persuade people he would also prove a responsible steward of the budget. During the campaign, President Hoover promised to balance the budget; indeed, he said he had always "insisted upon a balanced budget" and attributed the federal deficit to the "opposition leadership"—the Democratic majority that had prevailed in the House of Representatives after the election of 1930. Hoover said that if reelected, he would continue to stand against Democrats' "raids upon the Public Treasury."[30] Roosevelt tried to meet his opponent's pledge of austerity by promising that he would "approach" the goal of cutting ordinary federal operating expenses by 25 percent. But while scolding Hoover for profligacy, the governor also gave himself an out: when he said he would cut government expenditures, he exempted whatever expenditure was necessary to fulfill his promises of emergency aid in the Depression. "If men or women or children are starving in the United States—anywhere—I regard it as a positive duty of the Government—of the national Government if local and State Governments have not the cash—to raise by taxes whatever sums may be necessary to keep them from starvation. . . . There can be no extravagance when starvation is in question."[31] And indeed, once president, when pressed by reporters whether he aimed to balance the budget, he stuck to the same view: "It depends entirely on how you define the term, 'balance the budget.' What we are trying to do is to have . . . the normal Government operations balanced. . . . On the other hand, is it fair to put into that part of the budget expenditures that relate to keeping human beings from starving. . . . I should say probably not."[32] Roosevelt would have liked to balance the budget, but he had no intention of forgoing the New Deal to do it.[33]

Roosevelt's pledges of employment extended beyond mere relief of starvation. In the final phase of the 1932 election, Roosevelt set forth a plan for relief that only began with "No citizen shall be permitted to starve." He expanded on that commitment: "No mere emergency measures of relief are adequate. . . . Our goal, our unremitting objective, must be to secure not temporary employment but the permanence of employment to the workers of America." Thus the federal government would not only provide immediate relief from privation in cases where the local and state governments had failed, it would also employ Americans on public works and establish an advance plan of future public works to provide a reserve of available work in time of future need. Moreover, Roosevelt argued, the jobs offered by the federal government should be offered on good terms. Publicly provided jobs should pay well and entail a decent schedule, allowing employees to "earn enough so that they can buy the things that are produced, so that they can have the leisure for the cultivation of body, mind and spirit."[34]

To ensure that American voters knew about the New Deal's commitment to workers and their rights, the Roosevelt campaign depended heavily on the labor of the Women's Division of the

Democratic National Committee, headed by Molly Dewson, a longtime labor activist and social worker. Through this work, Dewson met first Eleanor Roosevelt and then Franklin, during the period after he suffered the onslaught of polio and before he reentered politics. The convalescing Roosevelt spent much of this time in his library, which Dewson "envied . . . for within reach from his roll chair were innumerable histories of America from its earliest days and those books were no interior decorators' effort." Dewson found Franklin as congenial, politically, as Eleanor. "I believed in the things he stood for."[35]

Dewson became part of the Roosevelt circle, assisting with campaigns and advising on matters relating to labor conditions. She successfully lobbied the governor to support a program of unemployment insurance and to appoint her fellow activist Frances Perkins as state labor commissioner, a post to which the earnest Perkins was well suited, whereas Dewson's talents lay more in the field of electioneering. One of Roosevelt's speechwriters, Charlie Michelson, regarded her as "the greatest she-politician" he knew.[36]

Specifically, Dewson knew how to write, publish, and distribute a political message, and in 1932 her Women's Division got Roosevelt's record and intentions as a jobs creator and a pro-labor candidate out into the country. Dividing the Democratic message into themes, Dewson and her staff designed a series of one-sheet leaflets, each addressing a single topic. She had 6 million of them printed, coded by color so campaign workers could easily identify and assemble them into comprehensive packets. The committee shipped these packets out in batches to precinct walkers, who would take them onto porches and into parlors or kitchens throughout the nation. Together with voters, Dewson's workers would sit and look at Roosevelt's programs for higher farm prices, lower tariffs, public electrical power, workers' rights, and publicly funded jobs. One sheet consisted entirely of reminders about the effectiveness of the TERA. In contrast to the absence of action from Washington, Roosevelt's unemployment program in New York had been widespread, providing prompt public aid to the unemployed "*not* through a dole but by Work Relief to the able-bodied, and Home Relief of food, shelter, clothing and supplies to the sick and helpless." Another sheet promoted the governor's record of support for workers in the form of shorter hours, higher wages, unemployment insurance, and protection for unions. Many people heard Roosevelt's speeches or read them in the papers, but still more found a description of his pledges of a New Deal jobs program coupled with better conditions for labor resting in their own hands, thanks to Dewson and her "grass-trampers."[37]

With these promises broadcast so widely, it would be essential that the New Deal public works programs go a long way, and soon, toward fulfilling pledges made to voters. Roosevelt felt keenly the need to make good on his promises; it was, he thought, essential to his aim of showing that democracy, as a political system, could meet the challenge of the Depression.[38] As Roosevelt told his aide Rex Tugwell, he knew he had raised Americans' hopes and he dared not fail them. Perhaps the bulk of the population had been desperate for nearly four years, but now that people had reason to expect better, the danger was higher: "Disappointed hope rather than despair, creates revolutions."[39]

Before Roosevelt had been in the White House three weeks, he consulted with congressional leaders to design a relief bill. The resulting Federal Emergency Relief Act of May 12, 1933, devoted $500 million to grants for states seeking to relieve unemployment. The Federal Emergency Relief Administration (FERA) created to administer these grants recapitulated the TERA both nominally, though eliminating its superfluous "temporary," and in terms of personnel: the head of the FERA would be TERA chief Harry Hopkins.[40]

Hopkins had few characteristics commonly associated with his profession of social work save moral intensity. He liked poker, horse racing, and drinking. A blunt speaker, he did not hold back in describing the "lousy" social conditions to which he objected. He had no trouble setting aside thoughts of what was most virtuous in favor of what was politically achievable. And he had proven himself capable of doing the job at the state level. Before the end of May, Roosevelt brought Hopkins to Washington to start the FERA. Initially, he was its only staff member, but he quickly began to assemble a team of advisors prepared to create federal jobs.[41]

Economic recovery began almost immediately with Roosevelt's inauguration; official data now peg the turnaround to March 1933.[42] The new administration's earliest actions to stop financial panics and preserve the banks of the nation restored confidence, ensuring that during the remainder of the month, Americans who had withdrawn money from savings accounts and gold from the Federal Reserve System brought it back, returning vault holdings to their former levels. Moreover, Roosevelt's policies helped ensure that people began to spend their money once more. To save the banks, Roosevelt used his presidential authority to stop the redemption of paper money for gold. The value of dollars in gold began to drop or, to put it another way, money became cheaper and Roosevelt's policies indicated it would continue to get cheaper still (and it did). With this expectation of inflation, Americans had good reason to believe that the money they had would be worth less in the future than it was at present, and so had reason to spend it while it retained a higher value.[43]

Even though the recovery began immediately and proceeded apace, the resumption of increased purchasing and producing did not instantly provide work and sustenance for the millions who needed it. The years of Depression had done more damage to the economy than could be readily undone. The FERA would step in to meet that need; so too would other recovery measures. The National Industrial Recovery Act of June 1933 allowed industries to organize and draft codes of fair competition that would establish minimum prices and wages; it also appropriated $3.3 billion, the bulk of which would be used by the Public Works Administration, which the statute also directed the president to establish. Roosevelt named Harold Ickes, secretary of the interior, to run the PWA.[44]

With the PWA's large budget came a devotion to large projects that would help to modernize undeveloped parts of the United States. Ickes and his officials thought chiefly about how PWA projects could develop the economy, not about how they could soonest put Americans to work. "The PWA," an agency report put it later, "acts somewhat in the nature of a bank or a large building and loan association."[45] Massive though it was, spectacular as its dams, bridges, libraries, airports, schools, and harbors might be, it did not do the work itself—nor, as Ickes said defensively after the PWA had been operating for a few months, did it set the pace of public works. By autumn, only about 250,000 laborers were employed on PWA projects, at a time when something like 10 million Americans remained unemployed.[46] The more than 300,000 men in the Civilian Conservation Corps's 1,466 camps made barely a dent in the jobless problem, either.[47] The FERA had issued more than $150 million in grants, reaching each of the forty-eight states, the District of Columbia, and the territories of Alaska, Hawaii, Puerto Rico, and the Virgin Islands, but it also estimated that around 4 million of the nation's families were still drawing public relief.[48] Critics both outside and inside the Roosevelt administration began to worry about the small size and slow rate of its jobs programs.[49] Some of the complaints came from the very constituents the programs were supposed to serve; one relief official quipped, "The Good Book says that the poor are always with us, but now they are against us."[50]

FERA field staff began reporting that leaving management of public works to the states produced predictably inconsistent and often bad effects. Different statehouses devoted varying levels of resources, from funding, to person-hours, to the administration of relief. Jacob Baker, director of the FERA's work division, and his deputy, Arthur Goldschmidt, observed that too many states were both underfunding projects and offering poor conditions to laborers. Hopkins issued orders that FERA grants could fund only projects that refused to employ anyone under the age of sixteen, for no more than eight hours a day or thirty-five hours a week, at a wage not less than 30 cents an hour. If the prevailing wage in the area was more, they should pay more. But the program remained frustratingly inadequate, piecemeal, and inequitable.[51]

Aubrey Williams, a social worker from Alabama who became a FERA field representative, traveled throughout the country looking at relief programs in action. Roadwork might well be the easiest job for a locality to undertake and might prove sufficient to meet the needs of work relief in some regions, but in densely populated cities there were more unemployed people than there was roadwork to do. Moreover, many of the jobless had unexploited talents beyond the strength and energy required for digging and paving. Williams suggested to his colleagues that the federal government begin to offer and fund a wider variety of public employment, including clerical and even artistic work.[52]

Listening to Baker, Goldschmidt, and Williams, among others, advocate a more systematic, broader, national program of public employment, Hopkins worried that a policy of that scope might fall afoul of organized labor. He dispatched Williams to consult the labor economist John Commons of the University of Wisconsin to see if there was any precedent for such work in the septuagenarian's capacious memory. Williams found the aged Commons still a chain-drinker of strong coffee and fully aware of how to find any relevant item in the stacks of offprints that lined his office. Commons pulled some studies published in the American Federation of Labor's own newsletter, noting that it was quicker and more efficient for governments to do their own work than to contract it to private firms. Hopkins believed that favorable comment from Samuel Gompers's own publication gave him license to proceed.[53]

On November 2, during a two-hour lunch meeting with Roosevelt, Hopkins pitched the idea of a federal jobs program with offices in all parts of the country in order to get Americans through the winter with work that could last them until PWA projects got up and running. Like Roosevelt, Hopkins regarded the dole as degrading. He preferred to hire unemployed people into jobs, preferably ones with some useful public consequence. Hopkins also hated means testing. Applicants for relief often had to pass the scrutiny of a social worker who, even with good intentions, needed to intrude into the most private aspects of a person's economic existence to determine eligibility for benefits. As Hopkins wrote, if Americans had not become so used to such interrogations, premised on a presumption of bad faith, "we should even now be astounded at our effrontery."[54] The program he proposed would have neither a dole nor means testing, he told Roosevelt, and could provide work to 4 million Americans. The president gave his approval; by evening, FERA staff had in hand the paperwork permitting Hopkins to take $400 million from the PWA's still-idle funds for his new agency. Williams was in New Orleans giving a speech on relief when he was interrupted by a staffer telling him he had a telephone call. Williams said to ask the caller to wait until the end of his talk. The staffer returned and told him, "Mr. Hopkins doesn't care what you are doing, come to the telephone." In addition to granting his immediate approval, the president had given Hopkins only a month to get the new program going and the FERA chief could lose no time.[55]

On November 8, Roosevelt and Hopkins announced their plans for federal jobs creation throughout the country. The new Civil Works Administration (CWA) would, as planned, get $400 million from the PWA and aim to hire 4 million Americans. Those employees would thus "become wage-earning, independent workers no longer dependent on charity." Hopkins amplified this point, saying Roosevelt wanted to ensure that no more Americans would "be forced to live under the auspices of relief organizations," subject to means testing: "Investigations will stop and we need no longer pry into the personal and private lives of these people."[56]

The CWA aimed to put Americans to work immediately in the hope they would spend immediately, and—consistent with Roosevelt's campaign message—it would also, by giving Americans what Hopkins called "real jobs at real wages," strengthen democracy as well as the economy. Hopkins said the CWA would move "millions of workers and their families from the level of relief to the real way of social and economic recovery, not only for individuals, for the nation. It raises their manner of living from charity to self-sustaining consumers of goods earned by their own labor." Moreover, "their increased income will flow from their hands into many channels of trade and industry wherever they live." The jobs would have to be public works, but modest ones—not ordinary city services that had to be supplied on an ongoing basis, but ways to develop a community: parks, playgrounds, roads, water and sewer infrastructure.[57]

On November 15, at a conference with governors and other officials, Hopkins and Roosevelt laid out the CWA's rules. Speaking extemporaneously, the president explained again that he wanted to get Americans off charity or direct relief. "When any man or woman goes on a dole, something happens to them mentally and the quicker they are taken off the dole the better it is for them during the rest of their lives." Reminding his audience again of the many people he wanted to employ and the large sum of money he meant to spend, he allowed for the possibility that people would accuse the White House of using the funds for political purposes. In the spirit of Hopkins's revulsion at investigation of public employees, he concluded, "I would like to have the general rule adopted that no person connected with the administration of this $400,000,000 will in any single case in any political subdivision of the United States ask whether a person needing relief or work is a Republican, Democrat, Socialist, or anything else."[58]

Less than a week later, CWA work began around the country, and on November 23, the infant agency issued checks to more than 810,000 workers. Federal checks were not nearly so common yet as they would shortly become, so to ease their acceptance, Roosevelt issued a personal communication urging that "banks throughout the country cooperate to the fullest extent, cashing these checks at par." A week later, 1.1 million Americans would be on CWA payrolls and by Christmas, nearly 3.4 million. The new agency would reach Hopkins's goal of 4 million employees early in January 1934. Such rapidity of employment was possible owing not only to the energy of Hopkins's staff but to their ingenuity in borrowing resources. In most cases the CWA adopted existing state relief offices rather than building new bureaucracies. It used the Veterans Administration as its accounting arm, and borrowed trucks and airplanes from the army to deliver material and paychecks.[59]

Because the money for CWA public works came from the PWA, Hopkins reasoned, he had to follow the same wage policy. For the purposes of determining rates of pay, the PWA divided the nation into zones. In recognition of the regions' different labor markets, wages varied across zones; for example, workers got 50 cents an hour in the North as against 40 cents an hour in the South. Even these calibrated rates of pay swiftly generated protests from private employers, who said they could not compete with what the CWA was offering and feared they would therefore lose employees to the federal government.[60] In addition, the CWA would mandate thirty-hour weeks, bar employees younger than sixteen, and set a preference for manual over machine labor to attain maximum employment. In December, the CWA would add a rule barring discrimination on the basis of race.[61]

Slightly more than one-third of the budget went to roadwork; with the addition of public buildings like schools and post offices, these works accounted for about half of CWA expenditure. The CWA leveled, repaved, and otherwise did work on about 255,000 miles of road, and repaired or constructed about 60,500 buildings, most of which were schools or colleges. The agency's laborers did other kinds of outdoor work as well, including erosion control, irrigation, laying out parks, and clearing ground for bigger projects such as airfields. Pest control and public health projects were major works as well; notably, almost thirty thousand CWA workers undertook malaria-control projects.[62]

To hire women and white-collar workers, Hopkins established a separate division, the Civil Works Service, funded out of the FERA's budget, with a flat 30-cent minimum wage that would rise to prevailing rates in the region of employment if those were higher. Because this was not PWA money, it could pay for useful work that did not fall into the traditional category of public works. Women did sewing, canning, and making mattresses for the Civil Works Service, work that would aid in the provision of food and shelter. Laborers also performed social-science surveys and other data analysis. Some worked in the arts. Music, particularly, was close to Hopkins's heart: "I cannot think of anything more important than music development in this country." If the nation could have more music in public places, he said, it "would encourage people to go out and sit around and talk and forget their troubles." The Civil Works Service sponsored small bands and symphony orchestras alike. It also funded visual arts; challenged on whether these warranted public funds, one administrator allowed, "Some people will believe it is a waste, but it has encouraged artists to continue, most of whom have been without employment. . . . It has encouraged many a young artist to develop . . . I believe it will bring about a renaissance in American art." About 190,000 Americans had Civil Works Service work by January.[63]

The programs grew, the projects proceeded, and the checks went out—also, the complaints came in. Perhaps it was inevitable that the CWA would err and prove vulnerable to bad actors because it grew so big so quickly; perhaps it was inevitable too that the CWA would breed dissatisfaction because as big as it grew, with 4.2 million workers on its payroll, nearly twice as many people nationwide remained unemployed. Even at its height, the CWA could not hire everyone who wanted one of its jobs. More, despite the president's promise of nonpartisan relief, complaints came in alleging political favoritism; Democrats, particularly, complained of Republicans, who remained in control of more than half of the state relief apparatuses.[64] Asked about this issue by reporters, Roosevelt acknowledged the scale of disapproval. "I should say those protests are equally divided between Republican politicians and Democratic politicians, and if I have had two or three hundred a day, probably Harry Hopkins has had two or three thousand a day."[65] The CWA investigated such allegations, and Hopkins was quick to remove state officials upon suspicion and refer serious matters for criminal investigation. Eventually, the Department of Justice convicted twenty-two people for various misuses of CWA funds—which might not have seemed like many, with 4 million employed, but it was enough to damage Hopkins's faith. He expressed dismay that under the circumstances, Americans would get up to such "petty chiseling," saying, "I suppose I'm naive and unsophisticated."[66]

Political attacks mounted. Al Smith, who had preceded Roosevelt as New York governor and Democratic nominee for president and had never quite forgiven Roosevelt for his success, derided the CWA as an effort to "afford an alibi for the incompetents in the Public Works Administration. . . . The Public Works crew can now take a long winter's nap, undisturbed by the necessity of issuing statements as to how many hundreds of millions of new projects have been approved, and as to why more men are not at work."[67] The Republican National Committee published a pamphlet called *C. W.A. Scandals: What Could You Expect* deriding the projects as "political set-ups to shovel out public funds, and put people on the public payrolls as a favor," the intended goal "to carry the 1934 elections."[68]

The CWA finally fell victim to its own success: as it employed more workers, it began to run out of money. Hopkins decreased hours, in the hope of keeping more people receiving some kind of check, and Congress voted further funds in a law of February 15, 1934, but only to give Hopkins time to wind down the program gradually. Demobilization began in the last week of February.[69] Now the relief administrator began to receive different complaints, this time about the imminent end of the jobs. But the experiment would soon stop. It would be better for the administration not to appear overly profligate in an election year. There was, moreover, a plausible case that recovery might proceed through other policies. Roosevelt had, at the end of January, just completed a nine-month project of devaluing the dollar to induce inflation and promote purchasing. The president therefore hoped that private employment would continue to improve, that the PWA would continue to hire more people, and that seasonal demand for labor in the farming industry would lessen, if not eliminate, the need for public jobs creation. By the end of March, Hopkins could declare the CWA officially terminated.[70] The administration would revisit in the fall the question of whether more job creation was necessary.[71]

Meanwhile, at the end of June 1934, Roosevelt set up a new advisory body, the Committee on Economic Security (CES), whose members included Hopkins, Perkins, Secretary of the Treasury Henry Morgenthau Jr., and Secretary of Agriculture Henry Wallace, to recommend legislation for the coming winter. Historians would later emphasize the role of the CES in drafting proposals for unemployment insurance and old-age pensions that eventuated in the Social Security Act of 1935, but Roosevelt also set the group the task of coming up with a new plan for "employment opportunities provided by government," including "large-scale public works."[72]

By the end of summer, a resumption of federal hiring looked likely. Unemployment grew again, and by September the relief rolls of the nation had over 4.7 million cases on them, more than any time since May 1933. Among other factors making Americans miserable, drought—the first wave of dry weather that produced the Dust Bowl—took its toll.[73] Notwithstanding these setbacks, the New Deal remained popular, and in November's elections the Democrats gained even larger majorities than they had in 1933 in both houses of Congress. Shortly afterward, Hopkins took members of his staff to enjoy a relaxing afternoon at the racetrack. In the car on the way, Hopkins burst out, "Boys—this is our hour. We've got to get everything we want—a works programs, social security, wages and hours, everything—now or never." He set the staff to work on proposals, and by Thanksgiving had plans in hand to take with him to Roosevelt's house in Warm Springs, Georgia. Hopkins's program leaked to the press, and newspapers reported that his wide-ranging ideas included the resettlement of drought- and Depression-struck farm families to better land, public housing, social insurance for those unable to work, and a new effort to give work to those who could—a "vast work program supplied by the Federal Government," as the *New York Times* put it.[74]

In January 1935, Roosevelt received the official CES report, and bills for new public works programs and a social security law went to Congress in the same month. In April, the president signed the first in a series of Emergency Relief Appropriation Acts, which allocated $4.88 billion for jobs programs. He would sign the Social Security Act in August, completing the CES agenda in just over a year after the committee's establishment.[75] Meanwhile, Roosevelt began assembling the new works agency. On April 28, 1935, he delivered the seventh in his series of fireside chats explaining that something like the CWA, only more durable, was about to begin. "I well realize that the country is expecting before this year is out to see the 'dirt fly.' " Speed in hiring would again be a priority—which raised the question of one unfortunate side effect of haste the CWA had generated: corruption. Anticipating this objection, the president acknowledged, "There are chiselers in every walk of life," and asked his listeners for their vigilance to help ensure the new program would be "the most efficient and the cleanest example of public enterprise." He asked to hear criticism. And as always, he explained that the purpose of a jobs program was not merely to provide economic stimulus, but to bolster the institutions of representation and "provide a smashing answer to those cynical men who say that a democracy cannot be honest and efficient." He noted the program would be immense: there might be "two hundred and fifty or three hundred kinds of work."[76] On May 6, Roosevelt signed an executive order creating the Works Progress Administration, or WPA, to employ "the maximum number of persons in the shortest time possible." He appointed Hopkins to run it.[77]

Hopkins and his staff would bring lessons from the CWA to the WPA. First, the budget, large as it was, was still not large enough to give jobs to all who needed them. Reluctantly, the New Dealers accepted a means test so the WPA could hire the more worthy candidates. Eager to hire, the CWA had outgrown its budget in a matter of months; the WPA could not repeat that error. As Josephine C. Brown, a Hopkins aide, wrote, "There was constant conflict between the desire on the one hand to do away entirely with the 'means test,' . . . and, on the other hand, the urgent necessity of making available funds go as far as possible in helping the most needy." One estimate reckoned that about 10 million Americans needed a job, which would require a budget of $10 billion, an enormous figure that Congress would not give.[78] (By way of perspective, recall that the PWA's budget stood at $3.3 billion.) A means test, however much loathing it inspired in Hopkins, Roosevelt, and the would-be workers who must endure it, had to become part of the WPA to keep its numbers down.

Second, mindful of how the CWA had been undone by charges of graft and partisan corruption in the state organizations, Hopkins's team planned a truly national agency. Each state would have an office with its own staff, and its administrator would be appointed in Washington. Eventually, New York City would have its own office; California would be divided into two; Washington, DC, Hawaii, and Puerto Rico would also get offices of their own. There could be no salary paid to anyone who was a candidate for election or working on a campaign.[79] The WPA had a Division of Investigation devoted solely to inquiring into allegations of fraud on its projects. This division had agents throughout the WPA, and shared information with the FBI, from whose veterans it drew many of its agents.[80]

Third, to deflect charges of extravagance and to forestall complaints from private employers, the WPA would also adopt a more modest wage scale than the CWA, setting a "security wage"—a rate of pay that would allow workers to afford a minimum standard of living. To assure that security, the WPA's administrators computed wages as monthly salary rather than an hourly rate.[81] Workers would be paid for time lost owing to weather or other circumstances out of their control. As before, administrators divided the nation into regions, ranging from the highest-earning region 1, including the industrial Northeast and the West, to the lowest-earning region 4, covering the Deep South. The salary scale extended from $19 a month for unskilled labor in region 4 to $94 a month for professional labor in region 1. Like the CWA, the WPA set rules for work conditions, barring the labor of people under sixteen years old and mandating an eight-hour day and a forty-hour week.[82] To account for the specific needs of the younger unemployed, of which officials reckoned there were about 5 million, the National Youth Administration (NYA) would work with, and to an extent within, the WPA; Aubrey Williams would run it.[83]

Early on, Hopkins issued orders barring racial discrimination on WPA projects, and appointed African American officials to positions in the agency, including Mary McLeod Bethune as director of the NYA's Division of Negro Affairs; thanks to

Bethune and her allies, the political scientist Ralph Bunche observed, "the NYA has probably been more successful than any other governmental agency in promoting full integration and participation of minority groups." In 1939, depriving someone of WPA employment or compensation on the basis of race would become a crime.[84] Largely owing to these efforts, black workers were overrepresented on WPA rolls in comparison to their proportion of the population.[85] The National Urban League's journal *Opportunity* praised the WPA in 1939, noting that "discrimination . . . has been kept to a minimum" and the program ensured that "in the northern communities, particularly in the urban centers, the Negro has been afforded his first real opportunity for employment in white-collar occupations."[86]

In terms of the scope of the works, the WPA echoed and amplified the CWA, extending its reach throughout the states and territories, covering useful projects that could be speedily mounted. Some were spectacular, reflecting the gifts of administrators who could put together many small projects to make something much larger than the sum of its parts, like Aquatic Park in San Francisco. Most were more modest, along the lines of CWA efforts: roads, parks, sidewalks. The ubiquity of the WPA was part of what made it simultaneously so beloved and detested; the WPA-built park in your city represented wise use of public funds while the WPA-built park in the neighboring town represented a waste of them. A public opinion poll of 1939 asked Americans to name "the greatest accomplishment" and "the worst thing" the Roosevelt administration had done; the WPA won both categories—although it was slightly more likely to rank best (28 percent) than worst (23 percent).[87]

Women could work for the WPA, if they were unmarried and willing to take a job considered appropriate to their gender. Whereas the WPA employed some millions of men at a time, it hired only a few hundred thousand women. New Dealers were not notably less likely than other Americans to think of families as headed by a man on whose ability to earn money a woman and children depended for their livelihoods.[88] As had been the case with the Civil Works Service, women primarily did sewing and canning work, producing the in-kind relief supplies necessary to clothe and feed the neediest people in the country. Some women who had never used sewing machines received valuable training with new machines when working on these projects, but many were applying the same skills they already knew.[89]

Men and women who worked for the WPA were often thrilled to have a job and the dignity of labor. They wanted to work, not to get relief. Writing to apply for WPA positions, they frequently put their request in terms of a right: "I deserve a job to work," they said. "We WPA workers want to work and be treated as workers." Yet they wanted that work to be more secure. Although policy makers thought of the FERA, the PWA, the CWA, and the WPA as representing progressive steps in the right direction toward full employment, to workers they represented an unnecessarily complex and inconsistent commitment to Roosevelt's "unremitting objective" of permanent employment. Sometimes they organized into unions; Roosevelt met the head of one. Sometimes the unions even struck for their rights.[90]

The pattern of spending on WPA works roughly matched concentrations of population, as you might expect of an agency designed to create jobs. The projects themselves served the purpose of economic development, and thus recognized the cornerstone New Deal principle of interdependence. For the nation to recover, to advance, its poorest sections and worst-off people must catch up; each was connected to all.

For the first few years of its existence, the WPA generally employed about 2 million Americans at any one time; it did not reach the size of the CWA. With the economy significantly improved by 1936, Roosevelt won reelection in a landslide. In a misguided and premature effort to show he would keep his promise of budget discipline as prosperity returned, Roosevelt cut WPA employment to around 1.5 million in the fall of 1937. The reduction of the WPA in 1937 repeated the error of eliminating the CWA in 1934; it was too soon to draw down the relief efforts. Although the economy had improved, it had not attained full recovery. A recession ensued, and the administration tried to make up for its mistake, reaching a peak of 3.2 million WPA workers in the following year.[91] Soon afterward, mobilization for military production began, and then in the latter part of 1940 came the draft. Before long, war jobs and spending far surpassed New Deal jobs and spending and wiped out the unemployment hangover remaining from the long slump that ended in 1933. The clear effect of wartime employment demonstrates that the WPA should have been much bigger much sooner to end the Depression (if you are considering its policies solely as a matter of stimulating the economy), and in this respect the jobs program demonstrated chronic weakness; the movement from the FERA to the CWA to the WPA, with the PWA slowly gaining strength all the time, did not amount to a smooth gradient upward. The administration should have started with a truly federal jobs program on a large scale immediately in the spring of 1933, and not reduced its size in 1934 or in 1937.[92]

But like Roosevelt's earlier efforts, the WPA aimed only secondarily at promoting rapid economic recovery; New Dealers meant it primarily to preserve and indeed exhibit American democracy. In this respect it succeeded all out of proportion to its level of spending. Here, its most effective programs—certainly in proportion to their expense, which was comparatively trivial—were those in the arts, which recapitulated and expanded the earlier CWA efforts in this field.

The WPA arts programs helped create a story of the United States and its many peoples that, to a considerable extent, Americans still remember. Federal Project No. 1 was a nationwide program for music, visual arts, writing, and theater, as well as surveys of the historical record. Symphony orchestras in Boston, Hartford, Providence, New York, San Francisco, and Los Angeles, among many other cities, had WPA funding. Theater projects included Orson Welles's extraordinary all-black *Macbeth* and an adaptation of Sinclair Lewis's *It Can't Happen Here.* Field workers for the writers' project traipsed through the southern states, interviewing survivors of slavery.

The project most expressly devoted to providing a portrait of the country in full was the American Guide Series. Employees of the WPA Federal Writers' Project traveled through all the states and territories and wrote up their findings. Even if the Depression prevented many Americans from undertaking leisure travel, the books could take you to all corners of the United States of America in your imagination, describing what you would see if someday you were able to go in person. They attempted simultaneously to provide useful information and a literary expression of history and culture. For example, the guide to Florida—described, accurately then, as the southernmost state—informed motorists of speed limits and other laws, where to find lodging and cinemas, and also advised travelers not to "enter bushes at sides of highway in rural districts; snakes and redbugs usually infest such places." In addition it offered reflections on the state's peculiar character: "Its northern area is strictly southern and its southern area definitely northern." Yet the peninsula was also like the rest of the nation: home to a variety of peoples and cultures; "Its melting pot is a brew of conflicting ideas." The guide touched on Seminole, Spanish, British, Cuban, and other cultures; on production of tobacco, turpentine, and citrus; on sightings of egrets, herons, manatees, and alligators; on tracks for horse racing and dog racing; on the descendants of enslaved people and the various kinds of white people, who called themselves Conchs in the southernmost part of the state and Crackers in the northern part. Contributors included the white journalist Stetson Kennedy and the black folklorist and fiction writer Zora Neale Hurston. The guide made no pretense at claiming a unitary Florida identity, yet it showed how the whole of the state was tied together—principally by its highways and their ubiquitous roadside attractions. Driving along, reading highway signs, you would find that "a great deal of early history is presented" and "the flora and fauna are similarly publicized," while "gastronomy and distance are combined in directional markers that announce 'II miles to Guava Paste' or '13 miles to Tupelo honey.'" The signboards also featured advertisements for a popular malaria cure—whose manufacturer complained to the guide writer that business had suffered since the New Deal introduced wholesale mosquito-abatement measures. In the matters of commerce, dining, and a need to avoid the inimical wildlife and endemic diseases, the common medium of the Florida roadside sign documented a culture that "introduces the Yankee to the Cracker and quickly establishes that the two have much in common."[93]

In the Florida guide, as in other state guides, the WPA writers were telling the story of the New Deal, implicitly but surely. The common carriageways on which all manner of travelers could meet and appreciate the wildlife kept at bay by flood and pest control, by roads and drainage, were the products of public works and a concrete manifestation of the interdependence that was a cornerstone principle of the New Deal.[94] Yet it was a ground held only tenuously in common, as Hurston—especially—recognized; she began some notes for research with an epigraph from a folk song she collected, which asserted an intent to commit a lynching "if I have to hunt Flordy over."[95] As the guide itself noted, for all that many peoples lived and depended on each other in Florida, "the Florida Cracker runs the courthouse and assesses, collects, and spends the tax money."[96]

In their recognition of the uneasy interdependence of various Americans with wildly differing histories, and their observation that all of them had recently come together on common ground built by the New Deal, the guides "ably illustrate our national way of life," as the president said, "yet at the same time portray the variants in local patterns of living and regional development."[97]

The graphic arts often did the same sort of work, seeking to depict a common American history while acknowledging a variety of experiences. Plains Indians in teepees and industrial laborers, farmers, and merchant seamen were all shown with a degree of abstraction that allowed them to be anybody and everybody. Maybe the style resulted from artists seeking to fulfill a commission to show American life while also trying to honor the sophisticated, more abstract schools of the time. It succeeded in giving Americans a sense of commonality in diversity. The designs that the artist Mary Blair would later produce for Walt Disney's "It's a Small World" owe much to this visual groping toward a depiction of the theme of interdependence, which underwrote the universalist elements of Roosevelt's own foreign policy in the Second World War.[98]

In the spring of 2020, the shelter-in-place orders required for public health robbed us of the shared spaces the New Deal built for us. We could not congregate in theaters, stadiums, or parks; we could not even stop to chat on sidewalks. Yet, if you stepped out onto the street where you live, you were just a few turns away from a national network of roads built by the New Deal, and you could follow them anywhere in the country. They made concrete the interdependence Roosevelt liked to talk about. And as the New Deal arts projects remind us, our interconnectedness is no less real even when it is intangible. We might usefully remember that basic underlying principle of the New Deal, an illustration of American and indeed international interdependence on which the preservation of democracy relies.

conclusion

In the spring of 2020, a reporter writing about Joe Biden said the longtime moderate was responding to the multiple crises confronting the country by repositioning himself as a "transformational crusader of the left" and pledging himself to an "FDR-size presidency." The economy needed more stimulus—something "a hell of a lot bigger," the candidate said. For the hardships confronting the nation now, including but not limited to the pandemic, unemployment, and human-produced climate change—"may not dwarf but eclipse what FDR faced," Biden said.[1]

Comparing a present-day remedy to the New Deal in terms of size has considerable merit. After all, one of the great lessons of the 1930s is that the New Dealers should have spent more money on hiring Americans sooner. In the event, it took the massive public jobs program that was mobilization for World War II to clear the nation's ledgers of unemployment. The biggest budget of Herbert Hoover's presidency ran to some $4.66 billion in 1932; the biggest New Deal budgets were not quite twice that, reaching

$8.42 billion in 1936 and $8.84 billion in 1939. The wartime budgets ran to ten times those sums, reaching $79.4 billion in 1943 and $98.3 billion in 1945. If Harry Hopkins had had the budget as WPA chief that he later had as chief of Lend-Lease, the New Deal might have been big enough to end the Depression much earlier.[2]

Yet despite its undersized budget, the New Deal reshaped American society more dramatically than costlier later interventions. The financial rescue package of 2008–9 amounted to perhaps five times the size (taking into account the proportions of the economy) of similar expenditures undertaken during the New Deal. But the government interventions of recent history, while immense in size, nevertheless fall short of the New Deal in terms of ambition.[3] The metaphor of "bailout" suggests the ship is sound; it has merely been swamped by a catastrophic swell and once the water has been expelled, it will again be seaworthy. Likewise "stimulus," which supposes the organism is healthy and merely needs a strong jolt of caffeine; or "pump-priming," which holds that the mechanism functions properly and the aquifer still yields plenty of water. By contrast, New Dealers did not assume the United States was basically sound as it stood, but sought to strengthen its structure—sometimes by substantially altering it.

In part, modern U.S. leaders' belief that even a dire crisis calls for no more than a bailout or stimulus is predicated on the success of the New Deal. The administrations of George W. Bush and Barack Obama could depend on the Federal Deposit Insurance Corporation (FDIC), an activist Federal Reserve; on social security payments and unemployment insurance—all products of the New Deal. That those institutions continued to function—and that more aggressive and quicker action forestalled a reprise of Depression levels of unemployment—appeared to vindicate the view that whatever restructuring the American economy might once have needed, the New Deal had long ago done it.

But that view has proved overly optimistic. Whole sections of the American population had not yet recovered from the financial crises of 2008 when the economic crisis of 2020 hit, nor did we counter the effects of climate change. The ongoing crises of our own time have, like the Depression, shown that we need something of the New Deal's effort to restructure the nation and the world.

The New Deal sought fundamentally to change the United States by introducing, in the phrase Roosevelt used, "the broadening conception of social justice" to American life.[4] The Depression revealed to a wider public the injustice and poverty long visited upon whole classes of Americans: tenants, laborers, farmers—as Roosevelt said in 1937, "one third of a nation"—and the New Deal sought to redress these issues. "Evil things formerly accepted will not be so easily condoned," the president said.[5] As he had stated in 1932, the nation could not address the present crisis by seeking "merely to restore"; it must "restore and at the same time remodel."[6] He recognized a difference of opinion between "those to whom this recovery means a return to old methods . . . and those for whom recovery means a reform of many old methods, a permanent readjustment of . . . our social and economic arrangements." He stood with the latter: "Civilization cannot go back."[7]

And even though the emergency needs or desperate politics of war could distort aspects of the New Deal (as we have seen in the cases of the TVA and the WPA), Roosevelt tried to turn the war more broadly into a global campaign for core elements of the New Deal, and particularly the four freedoms: freedom of speech and worship, freedom from fear and want. His administration ensured these aspirations informed statements of Allied war aims and the charters for postwar institutions.[8] "I have distinct reservations as to how good 'the good old days' were," he said in 1943. "I would rather believe that we can achieve new and better days."[9] The United States used its leverage as the provider of materiel to the Allies to ensure stronger institutions for the postwar world, designed—in the words of the Atlantic Charter—to provide "improved labor standards, economic advancement, and social security."[10]

Despite the sacrifices made in their name, these ideals failed of complete realization, as ideals tend to do. But they have not lost their power to inspire. In recent years, people attempting to meet modern crises have invoked them afresh, especially when seeking to conjure the scope of work involved in overcoming the world's climate crisis. The United Nations Environment Programme prepared a policy brief for a Global Green New Deal in 2009, and in 2019 Representative Alexandria Ocasio-Cortez and Senator Ed Markey introduced a resolution to both houses of the U.S. Congress "recognizing the duty of the Federal government to create a Green New Deal."[11] These efforts seek to create anew what Roosevelt called "the man-made world," and what we today might call the anthropocene, so that it might justly endure. The New Deal's effort, incompletely realized but doggedly pursued, of improving the economy by improving democracy, remains an outsized ambition even today.

notes

INTRODUCTION

1. "Inaugural Address, March 4, 1933," in *The Public Papers and Addresses of Franklin D. Roosevelt,* vol. 2, *The Year of Crisis* (New York: Random House, 1938), 11–17.

2. "One of the Outstanding Libraries of the Pacific Coast," *Davis Enterprise,* September 20, 1940, 1.

3. Jason Scott Smith, "New Deal Public Works at War: The WPA and Japanese American Internment," *Pacific Historical Review* 72, no. 1 (February 2003): 63–92; Richard Rothstein, *The Color of Law: A Forgotten History of How Our Government Segregated America* (New York: Liveright, 2017); Eric Schickler, *Racial Realignment: The Transformation of American Liberalism, 1932–1965* (Princeton: Princeton University Press, 2016).

4. Jason Campbell, "Lou Dobbs condemns Democrats for trying to 'push through the New Deal on the back of the American worker,' " Twitter, March 23, 2020, https://twitter.com/JasonSCampbell/status/1242200015180894208.

5. D. J. Judd, "Buttigieg on inequality in America," Twitter, December 11, 2019, https://twitter.com/DJJudd/status/1204959650476691456.

1. John Dos Passos, *1919* (Boston: Houghton Mifflin, 1932), 375.

2. Mauritz A. Hallgren, *Seeds of Revolt: A Study of American Life and the Temper of the American People during the Depression* (New York: Knopf, 1933), 4.

3. Eric Rauchway, *Winter War: Hoover, Roosevelt, and the First Clash over the New Deal* (New York: Basic Books, 2018), 140.

4. Paul Dickson and Thomas B. Allen, *The Bonus Army: An American Epic* (New York: Walker, 2004), 139, 171; D. Clayton James, *The Years of MacArthur,* vol. 1, *1880–1941* (Boston: Houghton Mifflin, 1970), 392, 398.

5. Dickson and Allen, *The Bonus Army,* 58, 66–67.

6. Theodore Joslin Diary, June 2, 1932, June 10, 1932, Herbert Hoover Presidential Library, West Branch, IA.

7. Dickson and Allen, *The Bonus Army,* 132–33.

8. Joslin Diary, June 17, 1932.

9. John Henry Bartlett, *The Bonus March and the New Deal* (Chicago: Donohue, 1937), 118.

10. Dickson and Allen, *The Bonus Army,* 135; Roger Daniels, *The Bonus March: An Episode of the Great Depression* (Westport, CT: Greenwood, 1971), 106, 127, 185; J. Cloyd Byars, "Washington Writer Views with Anxiety Conditions in America," *B.E.F. News,* July 9, 1932, 6; "Waters Outlines Road Ahead for New Organization," *B.E.F. News,* July 23, 1932, 1.

11. Joslin Diary, July 26, 1932.

12. James MacLafferty Diary, July 28, 1932, Hoover Institution Library and Archives, Stanford, CA.

13. Dickson and Allen, *The Bonus Army,* 162–63.

14. Dickson and Allen, *The Bonus Army,* 164.

15. James, *1880–1941,* 390.

16. James, *1880–1941,* 397; Dickson and Allen, *The Bonus Army,* 159.

17. Daniels, *The Bonus March,* 167.

18. Daniels, *The Bonus March,* 168; Donald J. Lisio, *The President and Protest: Hoover, Conspiracy, and the Bonus Riot* (Columbia: University of Missouri Press, 1974), 206.

19. Daniels, *The Bonus March,* 169; James, *1880–1941,* 401. On MacArthur's disobedience, see particularly Lisio, *President and Protest,* 190–225; also Charles Rappleye, *Herbert Hoover in the White House* (New York: Simon and Schuster, 2016), 376–79.

20. "Interview with General MacArthur by the Press at 11:00 PM, July 28, 1932," folder "World War Veterans Bonus March 1932–1959," Post-Presidential Subject File (hereafter PPSF), Herbert Hoover Presidential Library.

21. Daniels, *The Bonus March,* 181.

22. Joslin Diary, July 29, 1932.

23. Report for release September 12, 1932, with presidential statement of September 10, 1932, and report of September 9, 1932, in folder "World War Veterans Bonus March 1932–1959," PPSF; also "Father Lays Death of Ill Baby to Gas Used in B.E.F. Ejection," *New York Times,* August 10, 1932, 2.

24. Joslin Diary, August 21, 1932; "Of All Things," *New Yorker,* September 24, 1932, 18.

25. Joslin Diary, January 28, 1932.

26. Joslin Diary, July 24, 1932; on Hoover's reluctance to establish the RFC, see Gerald D. Nash, "Herbert Hoover and the Origins of the Reconstruction Finance Corporation," *Mississippi Valley Historical Review* 46, no. 3 (December 1959): 455–68.

27. Joan Hoff Wilson, *Herbert Hoover: Forgotten Progressive* (New York: Waveland, 1992), 151.

28. Folder "World War Veterans Bonus March 1932–1959," PPSF.

29. George Bothwell Brown, "Washington Sideshow," *San Francisco Examiner,* October 23, 1934, 32.

30. Herbert Hoover to Lawrence Richey, October 23, 1934, folder "World War Veterans Bonus March 1932–1959," PPSF.

31. Apart from a passive construction, that is: he wrote in his 1952 memoir: "Certain of my directions to the Secretary of War, however, were not carried out." Herbert Hoover, *The Memoirs of Herbert Hoover,* vol. 3, *The Great Depression, 1929–1942* (New York: Macmillan, 1952), 226–27.

32. "I Pledge You—I Pledge Myself—to a New Deal for the American People," July 2, 1932, in *The Public Papers and Addresses of Franklin D. Roosevelt,* vol. 1, *The Genesis of the New Deal, 1928–1932* (New York: Random House, 1938), 647–59.

33. Joslin Diary, June 28, 1932, July 1, 1932.

34. MacLafferty Diary, May 24, 1932, July 2, 1932.

35. Eric Rauchway, "The New Deal Was on the Ballot in 1932," *Modern American History* 2, no. 2 (July 2019): 203–6.

36. "Roosevelt Attacks 'Lopsided' Policies," *New York Times,* April 23, 1932, 6.

37. Franklin D. Roosevelt, *Government—Not Politics* (New York: Covici Friede, 1932), 28–29, 51.

38. Rexford G. Tugwell, *The Democratic Roosevelt: A Biography of Franklin D. Roosevelt* (Garden City: Doubleday, 1957), 349–50.

39. "Mills Challenges Roosevelt Fitness," *New York Times,* October 4, 1932, 3; "Statement on the Soldier's Bonus, October 4, 1932," box 13, Grace Tully Archive, series 4, Franklin D. Roosevelt Papers, Franklin D. Roosevelt Presidential Library, Hyde Park, NY.

40. "Hurley Declares Hoover Vindicated," *New York Times,* October 7, 1932, 10; "Hoover's Speech at Des Moines," *New York Times,* October 5, 1932, 18; "Stresses Aid to Credit," *New York Times,* October 12, 1934, 1.

41. "Roosevelt's Letter on the Bonus," *New York Times,* October 15, 1932, 8; "He Replies to Inquiry on Bonus," *New York Times,* October 18, 1932, 14.

42. "The Text of Governor Roosevelt's Speech to 30,000 in Pittsburgh Baseball Park," *New York Times,* October 20, 1932, 18.

43. Hoover, *Great Depression,* 229–30. See also Daniels, *The Bonus March,* 206.

44. Eleanor Roosevelt, *This I Remember* (New York: Harper and Brothers, 1949), 112–13; Frank Freidel, *Franklin D. Roosevelt,* vol. 4, *Launching the New Deal* (Boston: Little, Brown, 1973), 264–65; Press conference of May 16, 1933, in Maurine Beasley, ed., *The White House Press Conferences of Eleanor Roosevelt* (New York: Garland, 1983), 9.

45. "Against Bonus Marches," *New York Times,* April 23, 1933, E6.

46. Tugwell, *Democratic Roosevelt,* 346.

47. Nicholas Wapshott, *The Sphinx: Franklin Roosevelt, the Isolationists, and the Road to World War II* (New York: Norton, 2015), 215.

TWO: THE CLINCH RIVER

1. Donald Davidson, *The Tennessee,* vol. 2, *The New River: Civil War to TVA* (New York: Rinehart, 1948).

2. Michael McDonald and John Muldowny, *TVA and the Dispossessed: The Resettlement of Population in the Norris Dam Area* (Knoxville: University of Tennessee Press, 1982), 32; also Gordon R. Clapp, *The TVA: An Approach to the Development of a Region* (Chicago: University of Chicago Press, 1955), 15.

3. Davidson, *The New River,* 146.

4. Davidson, *The New River,* 177–78.

5. National Defense Act, June 3, 1916, 39 Stat. 166, 215.

6. Preston J. Hubbard, "The Muscle Shoals Controversy, 1920–1932," *Tennessee Historical Quarterly* 18, no. 3 (September 1958): 195–212.

7. Herbert Hoover, "Statement on Muscle Shoals Legislation," February 28, 1931, and "Veto of the Muscle Shoals Resolution," March 3, 1931, in *Public Papers of the Presidents of the United States, 1931* (Washington, DC: Government Printing Office, 1976), 115–16, 120–29.

8. "Text of Governor Roosevelt's Speech at Portland, Oregon, on Public Utilities," *New York Times,* September 22, 1932, 16.

9. "Roosevelt's Los Angeles Speech," *New York Times,* September 25, 1932, 32.

10. "Roosevelt's Los Angeles Speech."

11. E. F. Scattergood to FDR, January 31, 1933, Democratic National Committee Papers, Special File on Muscle Shoals, Franklin D. Roosevelt Presidential Library, Hyde Park, NY.

12. Paul K. Conkin, "Intellectual and Political Roots," in *TVA: Fifty Years of Grass-roots Bureaucracy,* ed. Erwin C. Hargrove and Paul K. Conkin (Urbana: University of Illinois Press, 1983), 3–34, esp. 25.

13. James A. Hagerty, "Alabamans Cheer Him," *New York Times,* January 22, 1933, 1; "Vast Shoals Plan Laid to Roosevelt," *New York Times,* January 26, 1933, 2.

14. Arthur M. Schlesinger Jr., *The Age of Roosevelt,* vol. 2, *The Coming of the New Deal* (Boston: Houghton Mifflin, 1959), 324.

15. Edgar Rickard Diary, February 4, 1933, Herbert Hoover Presidential Library, West Branch, IA.

16. Tennessee Valley Authority Act, May 18, 1933, 48 Stat. 58.

17. Barton M. Jones, "Norris Dam," *Scientific American* 152, no. 1 (January 1935): 24–26; Walter L. Creese, *TVA's Public Planning: The Vision, the Reality* (Knoxville: University of Tennessee Press, 1990), 168–81.

18. McDonald and Muldowny, *TVA and the Dispossessed,* 4.

19. North Callahan, *TVA: Bridge over Troubled Waters* (South Brunswick, NJ: A. S. Barnes, 1980), 31.

20. Ernie Pyle, "40,000-Square-Mile Area Being Revamped," *Pittsburgh Press,* December 27, 1935, 38.

21. McDonald and Muldowny, *TVA and the Dispossessed,* 181.

22. Ernie Pyle, "'Worn Out' Farm Land Reclaimed in Broad Social Plan of TVA," *Pittsburgh Press,* December 26, 1935, 18.

23. Earle Sumner Draper Jr., "The TVA's Forgotten Town: Norris, Tennessee," *Landscape Architecture Magazine* 78, no. 2 (March 1988): 96–100.

24. David E. Lilienthal, *TVA: Democracy on the March* (New York: Harper and Brothers, 1944), 52.

25. On TVA sponsorship of co-operatives, see Sarah T. Phillips, *This Land, This Nation: Conservation, Rural America, and the New Deal* (Cambridge: Cambridge University Press, 2007), 99–100.

26. Walter Kahoe, *Arthur Morgan: A Biography and Memoir* (Moylan, PA: Whimsie, 1977), 77–78.

27. Lilienthal, *TVA,* 95.

28. Ernie Pyle, "Norris Dam Amazes Writer," *Pittsburgh Press,* December 22, 1935, 17.

29. Ernie Pyle, "TVA to Save Big Area from Death Valley Fate, Reporter Says," *Pittsburgh Press,* December 23, 1935, 17.

30. Ernie Pyle, "Writer Finds Dams Form Small Part of TVA Rehabilitation," *Pittsburgh Press,* December 24, 1935, 7.

31. Aaron D. Purcell, *Arthur Morgan: A Progressive Vision for American Reform* (Knoxville: University of Tennessee Press, 2014), 171–72.

32. Clapp, *The TVA,* 19–20.

33. Stefan H. Robock, "An Unfinished Task: A Socio-economic Evaluation of the TVA Experiment," in *The Economic Impact of TVA,* ed. John R. Moore (Knoxville: University of Tennessee Press, 1967), 105–20, esp. 114. See also William M. Emmons III, "Franklin D. Roosevelt, Electric Utilities, and the Power of Competition," *Journal of Economic History* 53, no. 4 (December 1993), 880–907; Fred Bateman and Jason E. Taylor, "Franklin Roosevelt, Federal Spending, and the Postwar

Southern Economic Rebound," *Essays in Economic and Business History* 20 (2002): 71–83.

34. Marguerite Owen, *The Tennessee Valley Authority* (New York: Praeger, 1973), 215.

35. William E. Leuchtenburg, *The White House Looks South: Franklin D. Roosevelt, Harry S. Truman, Lyndon B. Johnson* (Baton Rouge: Louisiana State University Press, 2005), 42–43.

36. Draper, "The TVA's Forgotten Town."

37. Mardges Bacon, "Le Corbusier and Postwar America: The TVA and Béton Brut," *Journal of the Society of Architectural Historians* 74, no. 1 (March 2015): 13–40, esp. 24.

38. Davidson, *The New River,* 228–29, 237.

39. McDonald and Muldowny, *TVA and the Dispossessed,* 30.

40. Melissa Walker, "African Americans and TVA Reservoir Property Removal: Race in a New Deal Program," *Agricultural History* 72, no. 2 (Spring 1998): 417–28, esp. 425.

41. Joseph P. Lash, *Dealers and Dreamers: A New Look at the New Deal* (New York: Doubleday, 1988), 376–77.

42. Leuchtenburg, *White House Looks South,* 11.

43. Nancy L. Grant, *TVA and Black Americans: Planning for the Status Quo* (Philadelphia: Temple University Press, 1990), 109–13.

44. J. Saunders Redding, *No Day of Triumph* (New York: Harper and Brothers, 1942), 258–60.

45. Rexford Tugwell Diary, November 24, 1934, Franklin D. Roosevelt Presidential Library; Michael Vincent Namorato, ed., *The Diary of Rexford G. Tugwell: The New Deal, 1932–1935* (New York: Greenwood, 1992), 150.

46. "PWA Will Join TVA in Appeal to Save Cheap Power Plan," *New York Times,* February 24, 1935, 1.

47. Tugwell Diary, September 10, 1935; Namorato, *Diary of Rexford G. Tugwell,* 273.

48. Lash, *Dealers and Dreamers,* 268.

49. William E. Leuchtenburg, "Roosevelt, Norris and the 'Seven Little TVAs,' " *Journal of Politics* 14, no. 3 (August 1952): 418–41, esp. 420.

50. Leuchtenberg, "Roosevelt, Norris and the 'Seven Little TVAs,' " 420.

51. Lash, *Dealers and Dreamers,* 376–77.

52. Jess Gilbert, *Planning Democracy: Agrarian Intellectuals and the Intended New Deal* (New Haven: Yale University Press, 2016), 118.

53. Michael S. Sherry, *The Rise of American Air Power: The Creation of Armageddon* (New Haven: Yale University Press, 1989), 80.

54. Wilmon H. Droze, "The TVA, 1945–1980: The Power Company," in Hargrove and Conkin, *TVA,* 66–85.

55. Charles W. Johnson and Charles O. Jackson, *City behind a Fence: Oak Ridge, Tennessee, 1942–1946* (Knoxville: University of Tennessee Press, 1981), 3–14.

56. Johnson and Jackson, *City behind a Fence,* 150.

57. Johnson and Jackson, *City behind a Fence,* 159–60.

THREE: WINDOW ROCK

1. "National Historic Landmark Nomination for the Navajo Nation Council Chamber," 4–8, Records of the National Park Service, Records Group 79, National Archives and Records Administration, Washington, DC.

2. Peter Iverson and Monty Roessel, *Diné: A History of the Navajos* (Albuquerque: University of New Mexico Press, 2002), 7–29; Lawrence C. Kelly, *The Navajo Indians and Federal Indian Policy, 1900–1935* (Tucson: University of Arizona Press, 1968), 2–10.

3. Iverson and Roessel, *Diné,* 7–29, 51–62.

4. Francis Paul Prucha, *The Great Father: The United States Government and the American Indians* (Lincoln: University of Nebraska Press, 1995), 659–86, esp. 671.

5. For the foregoing account of the Navajo Nation, see Kelly, *Navajo Indians and Federal Indian Policy,* 62, 97–98, 103; also Robert W. Young, *A Political History of the Navajo Tribe* (Tsaile, AZ: Navajo Community College Press, 1978), 68–70. Fall's original orders and Work's amended version appear in "The Origin and Development of Navajo Tribal Government," *Navajo Yearbook* (1961): 371–411, esp. 393–97.

6. Lewis Meriam to W. F. Willoughby, March 30, 1927, in Donald L. Parman, ed., "Lewis Meriam's Letters during the Survey of Indian Affairs 1926–1927, Part II," *Arizona and the West* 24, no. 4 (Winter 1982): 350–61.

7. Lewis Meriam et al., *The Problem of Indian Administration* (Baltimore: Johns Hopkins University Press, 1928), 21–22, 41–42, 462.

8. Prucha, *The Great Father,* 921–37.

9. Kelly, *Navajo Indians and Federal Indian Policy,* 58.

10. On Collier, see Kenneth R. Philp, *John Collier's Crusade for Indian Reform, 1920–1954* (Tucson: University of Arizona Press, 1977); Frederick J. Stefon, "The Indians' Zarathustra," *Journal of Ethnic Studies* 11, no. 3 (Fall 1983): 1–28; and Frederick J. Stefon, "The Indians' Zarathustra, Part 2," *Journal of Ethnic Studies* 11, no. 4 (Winter 1984): 28–45.

11. Harold Ickes to Henry A. Wallace, January 3, 1933, Henry A. Wallace Papers, University of Iowa Libraries, microfilm, reel 18.

12. Lela Mae Stiles, *The Story of Louis McHenry Howe* (Cleveland: World Publishing, 1954), 231.

13. T. H. Watkins, *Righteous Pilgrim: The Life and Times of Harold L. Ickes, 1875–1952* (New York: Henry Holt, 1990), 202, 534.

14. John Collier, "At the Close of Ten Weeks," *Indians at Work,* September 15, 1933, 1–3; "Family Camp Work in Arizona and Montana," *Indians at Work,* September 1, 1933, 19.

15. Kelly, *Navajo Indians and Federal Indian Policy,* 156.

16. Watkins, *Righteous Pilgrim,* 536; "To the Indians and the Indian Service," *Indians at Work,* August 15, 1933, 1, 16; Donald L. Parman, *The Navajos and the New Deal* (New Haven: Yale University Press, 1976), 33–35. On the source *Indians at Work,* see Mindy J. Morgan, "'Working' from the Margins: Documenting American Indian Participation in the New Deal Era," in *Why You Can't Teach United States History without American Indians*, ed. Susan Sleeper-Smith et al. (Chapel Hill: University of North Carolina Press, 2015), 181–96.

17. Watkins, *Righteous Pilgrim,* 537; John Collier, "Public Works," *Indians at Work,* September 1, 1933, 3; "National Historic Landmark Nomination for the Navajo Nation Council Chamber," 6n5.

18. Kelly, *Navajo Indians and Federal Indian Policy,* 105; Watkins, *Righteous Pilgrim,* 544.

19. C. W. Collier, "Why Do Erosion Control Work?" *Indians at Work,* October 1, 1933, 11–15.

20. Watkins, *Righteous Pilgrim,* 537.

21. John Collier, "Indian Reservation Buildings in the Southwest," *American Architect and Architecture,* June 1937, 34–40.

22. Collier, "Indian Reservation Buildings in the Southwest."

23. John Collier, "The First Tribal Capital," *Indians at Work,* August 1, 1934, 6.

24. *Hearings Before a Subcommittee of the Committee on Appropriations, United States Senate, on the Interior Department Appropriation Bill for 1946,* May 7, 1945 (Washington, DC: Government Printing Office, 1945), 231.

25. F. R. Carpenter, "Establishing Management under the Taylor Grazing Act," *Rangelands* 3, no. 3 (June 1981): 105–15.

26. Sarah T. Phillips, *This Land, This Nation: Conservation, Rural America, and the New Deal* (Cambridge: Cambridge University Press, 2007), 200–204.

27. Kelly, *Navajo Indians and Federal Indian Policy,* 158–60.

28. Parman, *The Navajos and the New Deal,* 44–45.

29. Lawrence David Weiss, *The Development of Capitalism in the Navajo Nation: A Political Economic History* (Minneapolis: MEP, 1984), 101; Kelly, *Navajo Indians and Federal Indian Policy,* 160–63; Parman, *The Navajos and the New Deal,* 46, 49.

30. Marsha Weisiger, *Dreaming of Sheep in Navajo Country* (Seattle: University of Washington Press, 2009), 174–75.

31. Arthur M. Schlesinger Jr., *The Age of Roosevelt,* vol. 2, *The Coming of the New Deal* (Boston: Houghton Mifflin, 1959), 63.

32. Weisiger, *Dreaming of Sheep,* 97, 177.

33. Allan G. Harper, "The Indian Legislative Conference," *Indians at Work,* January 15, 1934, 3–8.

34. Philp, *John Collier's Crusade,* 140; Watkins, *Righteous Pilgrim,* 538; Prucha, *The Great Father,* 961.

35. Philp, *John Collier's Crusade,* 149.

36. Prucha, *The Great Father,* 960.

37. Prucha, *The Great Father,* 968; Donald L. Parman, "J. C. Morgan, Navajo Apostle of Assimilation," *Prologue* 4 (1972): 83–98, esp. 84–88.

38. Parman, "Morgan," 89; Parman, *The Navajos and the New Deal,* 72.

39. Emanuel Trocker, "The Navajo Indians and the Wheeler-Howard Bill," in *The Navajo as Seen by the Franciscans, 1920–1950: A Sourcebook,* ed. Howard M. Bahr (Lanham, MD: Scarecrow, 2012), 329.

40. Weisiger, *Dreaming of Sheep,* 179.

41. Parman, *The Navajos and the New Deal,* 167; Parman, "Morgan," 95–96.

42. Stephen J. Kunitz, "Factors Influencing Recent Navajo and Hopi Population Changes," *Human Organization* 33, no. 1 (Spring 1974): 7–16, esp. 11; Nancy Shoemaker, *American Indian Population Recovery in the Twentieth Century* (Albuquerque: University of New Mex-

ico Press, 1999), 34; Weiss, *Development of Capitalism in the Navajo Nation,* 118; Donald Parman, "Twentieth-Century Indian History: Achievements, Needs, and Problems," *OAH Magazine of History* 9, no. 1 (Fall 1994): 10–16, esp. 11.

43. Weisiger, *Dreaming of Sheep,* 223.

44. Andrew Needham, *Power Lines: Phoenix and the Making of the Modern Southwest* (Princeton: Princeton University Press, 2014), esp. 136.

FOUR: HUNTERS POINT

1. C. W. Short and R. Stanley-Brown, *Public Buildings: Architecture under the Public Works Administration, 1933–1939* (Washington, DC: Government Printing Office, 1939), esp. 638–39; William Lawson, *Achievements, Federal Works Agency, Work Projects Administration, Northern California; Jobs, 1935–1939* (San Francisco, 1939), 48.

2. Short and Stanley-Brown, *Public Buildings,* 185–87.

3. Lawson, *Achievements,* 79–80.

4. HOLC maps, Mapping Inequality project, University of Richmond, https://dsl.richmond.edu/panorama/redlining/; California Office of Environmental Health Hazard Assessment map of disadvantaged communities, https://oehha.ca.gov/calenviroscreen/sb535; Anthony Nardone, Joan A. Casey, Rachel Morello-Frosch, Mahasin Mujahid, John R. Balmes, and Neeta Thakur, "Associations between Historical Residential Redlining and Current Age-Adjusted Rates of Emergency Department Visits Due to Asthma across Eight Cities in California," *Lancet: Planetary Health* 4 (January 2020): e24–e31.

5. Gregory P. Downs, *After Appomattox: Military Occupation and the Ends of War* (Cambridge, MA: Harvard University Press, 2015); Heather Cox Richardson, *West from Appomattox: The Reconstruction of America After the Civil War* (New Haven: Yale University Press, 2008).

6. Eric Rauchway, *Murdering McKinley: The Making of Theodore Roosevelt's America* (New York: Hill and Wang, 2003), 71.

7. Bruce L. Mouser, *For Labor, Race, and Liberty: George Edwin Taylor, His Historic Run for the White House, and the Making of Independent Black Politics* (Madison: University of Wisconsin Press, 2011), 102–3.

8. Manning Marable, *W. E. B. Du Bois: Black Radical Democrat,* rev. ed. (London: Routledge, 2016), 90.

9. John Barry, *Rising Tide: The Great Mississippi Flood of 1927 and How It Changed America* (New York: Simon and Schuster, 1997), 368.

10. Nancy J. Weiss, *Farewell to the Party of Lincoln: Black Politics in the Age of FDR* (Princeton: Princeton University Press, 1983), 3–12; Eric Schickler, *Racial Realignment: The Transformation of American Liberalism, 1932–1965* (Princeton: Princeton University Press, 2016), 48.

11. Samuel O'Dell, "Blacks, the Democratic Party, and the Presidential Election of 1928: A Mild Rejoinder," *Phylon* 48, no. 1 (1987): 1–11.

12. Robert Chiles, *The Revolution of '28: Al Smith, American Progressivism, and the Coming of the New Deal* (Ithaca: Cornell University Press, 2018), 122.

13. Ralph J. Bunche, *The Political Status of the Negro in the Age of FDR* (Chicago: University of Chicago Press, 1973), 92; see also the analysis of public opinion polls in the later Roosevelt presidency in Schickler, *Racial Realignment,* 136–42.

14. "What We Want," *Chicago Defender,* October 20, 1928, A2; Allan J. Lichtman, *Prejudice and the Old Politics* (Chapel Hill: University of North Carolina Press, 1979), 151–52; Donald J. Lisio, *Hoover, Blacks, and Lily-Whites* (Chapel Hill: University of North Carolina Press, 1985), 50–63.

15. Eric Rauchway, *Winter War: Hoover, Roosevelt, and the First Clash over the New Deal* (New York: Basic Books, 2018), 112–13.

16. Holt Ross and Thomas E. Carroll, "Levees, Labor and Liberty," *American Federationist* 39, no. 3 (March 1932): 291–96.

17. "Mississippi River Slavery—1932," Dolph Briscoe Center for American History, University of Texas, Austin.

18. Rauchway, *Winter War,* 114. See also Richard B. Sherman, *The Republican Party and Black America: From McKinley to Hoover, 1896–1933* (Charlottesville: University Press of Virginia, 1973), 225–31.

19. *Statistical Abstract of the United States, 1933* (Washington, DC: Government Printing Office, 1933), 14–15. Disfranchisement obtained outside the former Confederate states as well; see Michael Perman, *Struggle for Mastery: Disfranchisement in the South, 1888–1908* (Chapel Hill: University of North Carolina Press, 2001).

20. On the characteristics of southern elections, see Devin Caughey, *The Unsolid South: Mass Politics and National Representation in a One-Party Enclave* (Princeton: Princeton University Press, 2018).

21. "I Pledge You—I Pledge Myself to a New Deal for the American People, July 2, 1932," in *The Public Papers and Addresses of Franklin D. Roosevelt,* vol. 1, *The Genesis of the New Deal, 1928–1932* (New York: Random House, 1938), 647–59; "Con. Speech, S.J.R. Draft," file no. 483, "Acceptance Speech on Receiving Nomination, 1932 July 2," Master Speech File, Franklin D. Roosevelt Presidential Library, Hyde Park, NY, http://www.fdrlibrary.marist.edu/_resources/images/msf/msf00493.

22. Joel Spingarn to Henry Morgenthau Jr., July 23, 1932, enclosing "Memorandum on the Negro Problem," and "Statement on the Negro Problem," Henry Morgenthau Jr. Papers, box 460, folder "FDR, 1929–1933," Franklin D. Roosevelt Presidential Library.

23. Franklin D. Roosevelt to Henry Morgenthau Jr., July 29, 1932, Morgenthau Papers, box 460, folder "FDR, 1929–1933."

24. Rauchway, *Winter War,* 115–16.

25. "Hoover or Roosevelt: Which?" *Chicago Defender,* October 22, 1932, 14.

26. "We Take No Side," *Atlanta Daily World,* October 30, 1932, 8A.

27. "Franklin Roosevelt Four-Square," *Pittsburgh Courier,* October 22, 1932, 10.

28. Weiss, *Farewell,* 32–33.

29. Ira Katznelson, *Fear Itself: The New Deal and the Origins of Our Time* (New York: Liveright, 2013), 241–42; Kathryn S. Olmsted, *Right out of California: The 1930s and the Big Business Roots of Modern Conservatism* (New York: New Press, 2015).

30. Gareth Davies and Martha Derthick, "Race and Social Welfare Policy: The Social Security Act of 1935," *Political Science Quarterly* 112, no. 2 (Summer 1997): 217–35.

31. Bruce J. Schulman, *From Cotton Belt to Sunbelt: Federal Policy, Economic Development, and the Transformation of the South, 1938–1980* (Durham: Duke University Press, 1994).

32. Franklin D. Roosevelt, "Address Before the Federal Council of Churches of Christ in America, December 6, 1933," in *The Public Papers and Addresses of Franklin D. Roosevelt,* vol. 2, *The Year of Crisis* (New York: Random House, 1938), 517–20.

33. Press Conference 125, May 25, 1934, 5, Presidential Press Conferences, Franklin D. Roosevelt Presidential Library, http://www.fdrlibrary.marist.edu/_resources/images/pc/pc0008.pdf.

34. Harvard Sitkoff, *A New Deal for Blacks: The Emergence of Civil Rights as a National Issue; The Depression Decade* (New York: Oxford University Press, 2009), 220.

35. Allan A. Michie and Frank Ryhlick, *Dixie Demagogues* (New York: Vanguard, 1939), 82.

36. Chloe N. Thurston, *At the Boundaries of Homeownership: Credit, Discrimination, and the American State* (Cambridge: Cambridge University Press, 2018), 47–52, 76.

37. Thurston, *At the Boundaries,* 77–93; Richard Rothstein, *The Color of Law: A Forgotten History of How Our Government Segregated America* (New York: Liveright, 2017), 65.

38. James T. Patterson, *The New Deal and the States: Federalism in Transition* (Westport, CT: Greenwood, 1981), esp. 205–7.

39. Weiss, *Farewell,* 207–8.

40. Weiss, *Farewell,* 210.

41. Weiss, *Farewell,* 214–18.

42. Robert C. Weaver, "The Adviser on Negro Affairs," in *Annual Report of the Secretary of the Interior for 1936* (Washington, DC: Government Printing Office, 1936), 49; Jill Watts, *The Black Cabinet: The Untold Story of African Americans and Politics in the Age of Roosevelt* (New York: Grove, 2020), Kindle, loc. 1344–1684.

43. Watts, *Black Cabinet,* loc. 1744.

44. Watts, *Black Cabinet,* loc. 1952.

45. Eugene Davidson, "The Black Cabinet in the New Deal," *Philadelphia Tribune,* March 29, 1934, 5.

46. Anthony J. Badger, "How Did the New Deal Change the South?" in *New Deal/New South: An Anthony J. Badger Reader,* ed. James C. Cobb (Fayetteville: University of Arkansas Press, 2007), 31–44, esp. 38.

47. Watts, *Black Cabinet,* loc. 2571–82.

48. John B. Kirby, *Black Americans in the Roosevelt Era: Liberalism and Race* (Knoxville: University of Tennessee Press, 1980), 111–20; Watt, *Black Cabinet,* loc. 3014.

49. "Industrial Unions and the Negro Worker," *Crisis,* September 1936, 273.

50. Schickler, *Racial Realignment,* 66–67.

51. David M. Chalmers, *Hooded Americanism: The History of the Ku Klux Klan* (Durham: Duke University Press, 1987), 320–21.

52. Badger, "How Did the New Deal Change the South?" 36; see also Robert Zieger, *The CIO, 1935–1955* (Chapel Hill: University of North Carolina Press, 1995).

53. Katznelson, *Fear Itself,* 267–75.

54. Sidney M. Milkis, "Franklin D. Roosevelt and the Transcendence of Partisan Politics," *Political Science Quarterly* 100, no. 3 (Autumn 1985): 479–504, esp. 490.

55. Susan Dunn, *Roosevelt's Purge: How FDR Fought to Change the Democratic Party* (Cambridge, MA: Belknap Press of Harvard University Press, 2010).

56. Frank Murphy to Franklin D. Roosevelt, December 2, 1932, President's Secretary's File, folder "Frank Murphy," Franklin D. Roosevelt Presidential Library.

57. Sidney Fine, *Frank Murphy: The Washington Years* (Ann Arbor: University of Michigan Press, 1984), 79.

58. Robert K. Carr, *Federal Protection of Civil Rights: Quest for a Sword* (Ithaca: Cornell University Press, 1947), 24; Henry Putzel Jr., "Federal Civil Rights Enforcement: A Current Appraisal," *University of Pennsylvania Law Review* 99, no. 4 (January 1951): 439–54, esp. 441n15.

59. DOJ Circular no. 2256, May 21, 1940, Thomas J. Dodd Papers, University of Connecticut Digital Library, http://archives.lib.uconn.edu.

60. Press Conference 649-A, June 5, 1940, Presidential Press Conferences, Franklin D. Roosevelt Presidential Library, http://www.fdrlibrary.marist.edu/archives/collections/franklin/.

61. Brief for the United States, *US v. Classic,* case no. 618, Supreme Court of the United States, October Term, 1940.

62. *United States v. Classic,* 313 U.S. 299 (1941), at 313.

63. Kevin J. McMahon, *Reconsidering Roosevelt on Race: How the Presidency Paved the Road to "Brown"* (Chicago: University of Chicago Press, 2003), 153–54.

64. Brief for petitioner, *Smith v. Allwright,* case no. 51, Supreme Court of the United States, October Term, 1943. On the Civil Rights Section's support for labor rights, see Risa L. Goluboff, *The Lost Promise of Civil Rights* (Cambridge, MA: Harvard University Press, 2007).

65. Ralph J. Bunche, "Conceptions and Ideologies of the Negro Problem, with Some Random Observations in Plain and Fancy Thinking," March 5, 1940, and Ralph J. Bunche, "Extended Memorandum on the Programs, Ideologies, Tactics and Achievements of Negro Betterment and Interracial Organizations," June 1, 1940, Carnegie-Myrdal Research Memoranda, Schomburg Center of the New York Public Library, microfilm, reel 1.

66. Bunche, "Conceptions and Ideologies."

67. Guido van Rijn, *Roosevelt's Blues: African-American Blues and Gospel Songs on FDR* (Jackson: University of Mississippi Press, 1997), 194–95.

68. Alexandria Ocasio-Cortez, interview with Briahna Gray at the South by Southwest Festival, March 10, 2019, https://www.youtube.com/watch?v=JU-SE5eNto4; "Recognizing the Duty of the Federal Government to Create a Green New Deal," House Resolution 109, February 7, 2019, https://www.congress.gov/116/bills/hres109/BILLS-116hres109ih.pdf.

FIVE: THE STREET WHERE YOU LIVE

1. *Final Report on the WPA Program* (Washington, DC: Government Printing Office, 1946), 50.

2. American Society of Planning Officials, "Sidewalks in the Suburbs," February 1957, https://www.planning.org/pas/reports/report95.htm.

3. Laura Bliss, "Drivers Not Wanted on Oakland's Slow Streets," City Lab, April 17, 2020, https://www.citylab.com/transportation/2020/04/slow-streets-oakland-car-free-roads-pedestrians-covid-19/609961/.

4. *Final Report on the WPA Program,* 122.

5. *Final Report on the WPA Program,* 50–53.

6. Alexander J. Field, *A Great Leap Forward: 1930s Depression and U.S. Economic Growth* (New Haven: Yale University Press, 2011), 40; see

also discussion of how the New Deal built the "first national road network" (72).

7. Lloyd E. Blauch, *Vocational Rehabilitation of the Physically Disabled* (Washington, DC: Government Printing Office, 1938), 10.

8. "Report and Recommendations of the Committee on Economic Security," *Monthly Labor Review* 40, no. 2 (February 1935): 304–23.

9. Daniel Holland, "Franklin D. Roosevelt's Shangri-La: Foreshadowing the Independent Living Movement in Warm Springs, Georgia, 1926–1945," *Disability and Society* 21, no. 5 (August 2006): 513–35.

10. On the New Deal orientation to consumerism, see Meg Jacobs, *Pocketbook Politics: Economic Citizenship in Twentieth-Century America* (Princeton: Princeton University Press, 2005).

11. "Jobs for Four Million in Place of Relief," *New York Times,* November 19, 1933, XX1.

12. Robert E. Sherwood, *Roosevelt and Hopkins: An Intimate History,* rev. ed. (New York: Harper and Brothers, 1950), 57.

13. "A New Deal for the Arts," National Archives, n.d., https://www.archives.gov/exhibits/new_deal_for_the_arts/celebrating_the_people1.html.

14. See *University of Michigan School of Education Staff Bulletin* (1937): 5.

15. "The Uses of CWA Art," *Washington Post,* February 9, 1934, 8.

16. Nick Taylor, *American-Made: The Enduring Legacy of the WPA, When FDR Put America to Work* (New York: Bantam Books, 2008), 274.

17. W. A. Warn, "Roosevelt Asks $20,000,000 for Jobless," *New York Times,* August 29, 1931, 1; Franklin D. Roosevelt, "New York State Takes the Lead in the Relief of the Unemployed, August 28, 1931," in *The Public Papers and Addresses of Franklin D. Roosevelt,* vol. 1, *The Genesis of the New Deal, 1928–1932* (New York: Random House, 1938), 457–68.

18. "Seek Wider Season for Building Work," *New York Times,* May 10, 1925, 10; *Report of the President's Conference on Unemployment* (Washington, DC: Government Printing Office, 1921), 96–98; James H. Shideler, *Farm Crisis, 1919–1923* (Berkeley: University of California Press, 1957), 162–63.

19. Herbert Hoover, "Statement on Public vs. Private Financing of Relief Efforts, February 3, 1931," in *Public Papers of the Presidents of the United States, 1931* (Washington, DC: Government Printing Office, 1976), 54–58.

20. Herbert Hoover, "Radio Address to the Nation on Unemployment Relief, October 18, 1931," in *Public Papers of the Presidents of the United States, 1931,* 487–91. On Hoover's opposition to public works, see also Joan Hoff Wilson, *Herbert Hoover: Forgotten Progressive* (New York: HarperCollins, 1975), esp. 150.

21. Roosevelt, "New York State Takes the Lead."

22. Roosevelt, "New York State Takes the Lead"; and Frank Freidel, *Franklin D. Roosevelt: The Triumph* (Boston: Little, Brown, 1956), 219–23.

23. Freidel, *Franklin D. Roosevelt,* 219–23.

24. William E. Leuchtenburg, *The American President: From Teddy Roosevelt to Bill Clinton* (New York: Oxford University Press, 2015), 139.

25. Franklin D. Roosevelt, *Government—Not Politics* (New York: Covici Friede, 1932), 27–29.

26. Franklin D. Roosevelt, "Social Justice through Social Action, October 2, 1932," in *Genesis of the New Deal,* 771–80.

27. Franklin D. Roosevelt, "Railroad Mesh Is the Warp on Which Our Economic Web Is Largely Fashioned, September 17, 1932," in *Genesis of the New Deal,* 711–23.

28. Roosevelt used the word often, but see particularly "Restored and Rehabilitated Agriculture, September 14, 1932," in *Genesis of the New Deal,* 693–711.

29. "Text of Gov. Roosevelt's Farm Relief Speech at Atlanta," *New York Times,* October 25, 1932, 14.

30. Herbert Hoover, "Address Accepting the Republican Presidential Nomination, August 11, 1932," in *Public Papers of the Presidents of the United States, 1932–33* (Washington, DC: Government Printing Office, 1977), 357–76.

31. Franklin D. Roosevelt, "Campaign Address on the Federal Budget, October 19, 1932," in *Genesis of the New Deal,* 795–812.

32. Press Conference 5, March 22, 1933, Press Conferences of Franklin D. Roosevelt, 1933–1945, Franklin D. Roosevelt Presidential Library, http://www.fdrlibrary.marist.edu/_resources/images/pc/pc0184.pdf.

33. On frugality in the New Deal, see Anthony J. Badger, *FDR: The First Hundred Days* (New York: Hill and Wang, 2008); and Julian E. Zelizer, "The Forgotten Legacy of the New Deal: Fiscal Conservatism and the Roosevelt Administration, 1933–1938," *Presidential Studies Quarterly* 30, no. 2 (June 2000): 331–58.

34. "'We Are through with "Delay"; We Are through with "Despair"; We Are Ready, and Waiting for Better Things,' Campaign Address on a Program for Unemployment and Long-range Planning, October 31, 1932," in *Genesis of the New Deal,* 842–55.

35. Mary Williams "Molly" Dewson, "An Aid to the End," 1–5, typescript, Mary Williams Dewson Papers, A-60, Radcliffe Library, Harvard University, Cambridge, MA. See also Susan Ware, *Partner and I: Molly Dewson, Feminism, and New Deal Politics* (New Haven: Yale University Press, 1987), 32–57; and, on Roosevelt's reading habits, James Tobin, *The Man He Became: How FDR Defied Polio to Win the Presidency* (New York: Simon and Schuster, 2013), 170–75.

36. Charles Michelson, *The Ghost Talks* (New York: G. P. Putnam's Sons, 1944), 26.

37. Dewson, "An Aid to the End," some flyers reproduced between typescript pages 63 and 64 and more between 64 and 65.

38. Eric Rauchway, "The New Deal Was on the Ballot in 1932," *Modern American History* 2, no. 2 (July 2019): 201–13.

39. Rexford G. Tugwell, "Transition: Hoover to Roosevelt, 1932–1933," *Centennial Review,* 9 no. 2 (Spring 1965): 160–91, esp. 187.

40. Federal Emergency Relief Act, May 12, 1933, 48 Stat. 55. Funds for the FERA would come from the Reconstruction Finance Corporation, a 1932 creation of Congress patterned on the War Finance Corporation and devoted in Hoover's last year of office chiefly to bailing out banks. Hoover reluctantly acquiesced in its creation and resisted its operation. See Gerald Nash, "Herbert Hoover and the Origins of the Reconstruction Finance Corporation," *Mississippi Valley Historical Review* 46, no. 3 (December 1959): 455–68.

41. On Hopkins, see Sherwood, *Roosevelt and Hopkins;* also Ernest K. Lindley, *The Roosevelt Revolution: A History of the New Deal* (New York: Viking, 1933), 294.

42. *Historical Statistics of the United States, Earliest Times to the Present, Millennial Edition,* ed. Susan B. Carter et al., vol. 3, *Part C: Economic Structure and Performance* (Cambridge: Cambridge University Press, 2006), 79, table Cb 5–8.

43. Eric Rauchway, *The Money Makers: How Roosevelt and Keynes Ended the Depression, Defeated Fascism, and Secured a Prosperous Peace* (New York: Basic Books, 2015), esp. 39–72.

44. National Industrial Recovery Act, June 16, 1933, 48 Stat. 195. On the effect of the NRA, see Gauti B. Eggertsson, "Was the New Deal Contractionary?" *American Economic Review* 102, no. 1 (February 2012): 524–55.

45. C. W. Short and R. Stanley-Brown, *Public Buildings: A Survey of Architecture of Projects Constructed by Federal and Other Governmental Bodies between the Years 1933 and 1939* (Washington, DC: Government Printing Office, 1939), vi.

46. "Employment in Public Works," *New York Times,* December 3, 1933, 2.

47. "125,000 Will Quit Forest Camp Jobs," *New York Times,* October 1, 1933, N1.

48. *Monthly Report of the Federal Emergency Relief Administration,* August 1933 (Washington, DC: Government Printing Office, 1933), 8, 14.

49. Jason Scott Smith, *Building New Deal Liberalism: The Political Economy of Public Works, 1933–1956* (Cambridge: Cambridge University Press, 2006), 49–53.

50. Forrest A. Walker, *The Civil Works Administration: An Experiment in Federal Work Relief, 1933–1934* (New York: Garland, 1979), 26–27.

51. *Monthly Report of the Federal Emergency Relief Administration, July 1933* (Washington, DC: Government Printing Office, 1933), 11.

52. Walker, *Civil Works Administration,* 30.

53. See, for example, J. R. Commons, "A Comparison of Day Labor and Contract System on Municipal Works, V," *American Federationist* 4, no. 3 (May 1897): 49–51; J. R. Commons, "A Comparison of Day Labor and Contract System on Municipal Works, XIII," *American Federationist* 4, no. 11 (January 1898): 252–53; F. Herbert Snow, "A Comparison of Day Labor and Contract System on Municipal Works," *American Federationist* 6, no. 6 (August 1899): 124–26; Sherwood, *Roosevelt and Hopkins,* 51.

54. Walker, *Works Administration,* 28.

55. Walker, *Works Administration,* 34–35; Sherwood, *Roosevelt and Hopkins,* 51.

56. "4,000,000 Idle to Be Hired; Works Plan Bars 'Charity,' " *New York Times,* November 9, 1933, 1.

57. "Jobs for Four Million In Place of Relief."

58. Franklin D. Roosevelt, "Extemporaneous Speech to C. W. A. Conference in Washington, November 15, 1933," in *The Public Papers and Addresses of Franklin D. Roosevelt,* vol. 2, *The Year of Crisis* (New York: Random House, 1938), 468–71.

59. "Asks Banks to Speed Public Works Checks," *New York Times,* November 24, 1933, 30; Walker, *Civil Works Administration,* 43, 67, 54.

60. On southern protests at New Deal wage rates, see particularly Katherine Rye Jewell, *Dollars for Dixie: Business and the Transformation of Conservatism in the Twentieth Century* (Cambridge: Cambridge University Press, 2017).

61. *Federal Civil Works Administration, Rules and Regulations,* no. 1, November 15, 1933 (Washington, DC: Government Printing Office, 1933), 4; *Federal Civil Works Administration, Rules and Regulations,* no. 10, December 13, 1933 (Washington, DC: Government Printing Office, 1933), 4; Walker, *Civil Works Administration,* 65.

62. Pamela Brown, *Analysis of Civil Works Program Statistics* (Washington, DC: Works Progress Administration, 1939), 10; Walker, *Civil Works Administration,* 95.

63. Walker, *Civil Works Administration,* 97–100.

64. Walker, *Civil Works Administration,* 111.

65. Press Conference 91, January 24, 1934, Press Conferences of Franklin D. Roosevelt, 1933–1945, Franklin D. Roosevelt Presidential Library, http://www.fdrlibrary.marist.edu/_resources/images/pc/pc0002.pdf, 104.

66. Walker, *Civil Works Administration,* 107, 129.

67. Alfred E. Smith, "Civil Works," *New Outlook,* December 1934, 11–12.

68. "Republican Book Opens CWA Attack," *New York Times,* February 9, 1934, 8.

69. *Monthly Report of the Federal Emergency Relief Administration,* February 1934 (Washington, DC: Government Printing Office, 1934), 3.

70. *Monthly Report of the Federal Emergency Relief Administration,* April 1934 (Washington, DC: Government Printing Office, 1934), 2.

71. Press Conference 91, January 24, 1934, http://www.fdrlibrary.marist.edu/_resources/images/pc/pc0002.pdf, 103.

72. "Roosevelt Cabinet Group to Gather National Data for Wide Social Program," *New York Times,* June 30, 1934, 1. On the relation of the WPA to the CES, see Steven Attewell, *People Must Live by Work: Direct Job Creation in America, from FDR to Reagan* (Philadelphia: University of Pennsylvania Press, 2018).

73. *Monthly Report of the Federal Emergency Relief Administration,* October 1934 (Washington, DC: Government Printing Office, 1934), 1.

74. "Roosevelt Maps Work-Relief Plan," *New York Times,* December 2, 1934, 1; Delbert Clark, "Flurry Over Hopkins Finds His 'EPIA' at Work," *New York Times,* December 2, 1934, E1; Sherwood, *Roosevelt and Hopkins,* 65.

75. Josephine Chapin Brown, *Public Relief, 1929–1939* (New York: Henry Holt, 1940), 302.

76. Franklin D. Roosevelt, "The First 'Fireside Chat' of 1935, April 28, 1935," in *The Public Papers and Addresses of Franklin D. Roosevelt,* vol. 4, *The Court Disapproves, 1935* (New York: Random House, 1938), 132–40, esp. 137.

77. Franklin D. Roosevelt, "Creation of Machinery for the Works Progress Administration, May 6, 1935," in *The Court Disapproves,* 163–69.

78. Brown, *Public Relief,* 158.

79. Arthur W. Macmahan, John D. Millett, and Gladys Ogden, *The Administration of Federal Work Relief* (Chicago: Public Administration Service, 1941), 200, 282; Lewis Meriam, *Relief and Social Security* (Washington, DC: Brookings Institution Press, 1946), 364. On the special place of New York City in the New Deal, see Mason B. Williams, *City of Ambition: FDR, La Guardia, and the Making of Modern New York* (New York: Norton, 2013).

80. *Final Report on the WPA Program,* 82–83.

81. Macmahan, Millett, and Ogden, *Administration,* 149.

82. Franklin D. Roosevelt, Executive Order 7046, May 20, 1935, Executive Orders and Presidential Proclamations, FDR Library, http://www.fdrlibrary.marist.edu/_resources/images/eo/e00029.pdf.

83. Macmahan, Millett, and Ogden, *Administration,* 85.

84. Joint Resolution Making an Additional Appropriation for Relief, February 4, 1939, 53 Stat. 507; Donald S. Howard, *The WPA and Federal Relief Policy* (New York: Russell Sage Foundation, 1943), 286.

85. Ralph J. Bunche, *The Political Status of the Negro in the Age of FDR* (Chicago: University of Chicago Press, 1973), 624; Richard Sterner, Lenore A. Epstein, Ellen Winston, et al., *The Negro's Share: A Study of Income, Consumption, Housing and Public Assistance* (New York: Harper and Brothers, 1943), 240. Black workers were so overrepresented in northern states that it outweighed their slighter underrepresentation in southern ones.

86. "The WPA," *Opportunity* 17, no. 2 (February 1939): 34–35.

87. "Relief Top Issue," *New York Times,* June 4, 1939, 27; Howard, *The WPA and Federal Relief Policy,* 105.

88. On the New Deal and the formation of identity, see Margot Canaday, *The Straight State: Sexuality and Citizenship in Twentieth-Century America* (Princeton: Princeton University Press, 2009).

89. *Final Report on the WPA Program,* 59, 68. See also Linda Gordon, *Pitied but Not Entitled: Single Mothers and the History of Welfare, 1890–1935* (New York: Free Press, 1994).

90. Elna C. Green, "Relief from Relief: The Tampa Sewing-Room Strike of 1937 and the Right to Welfare," *Journal of American History* 95, no. 4 (March 2009): 1012–37; Chad Alan Goldberg, "Contesting the Status of Relief Workers during the New Deal: The Workers Alliance of America and the Works Progress Administration, 1935–1941," *Social Science History* 29, no. 3 (Fall 2005): 337–71; Matt Perry, *Bread and Work: The Experience of Unemployment, 1918–1939* (London: Pluto, 2000), 155–58.

91. *Final Report on the WPA Program,* 28–29. Multiple policy errors probably contributed to the recession, including also a tighter monetary policy adopted at the same time; see Douglas A. Irwin, "Gold Sterilization and the Recession of 1937–1938," *Financial History Review* 19, no. 3

(December 2012): 249–67; also Gauti B. Eggertsson and Benjamin Pugsley, "The Mistake of 1937: A General Equilibrium Analysis," *Monetary and Economic Studies* (December 2006): 151–207.

92. For an economic history account, see Christina D. Romer, "What Ended the Great Depression?" *Journal of Economic History* 52, no. 4 (December 1992): 757–84; also Christina D. Romer, "Lessons from the Great Depression for Policy Today," teach-in paper, March 11, 2013, https://eml.berkeley.edu/~cromer/Lectures/Lessons%20from%20 the%20Great%20Depression%20for%20Policy%20Today%20Written.pdf. On persistent unemployment, see Gabriel P. Mathy, "Hysteresis and Persistent Long-Term Unemployment: The American Beveridge Curve of the Great Depression and World War II," *Cliometrica* 12, no. 1 (January 2018): 127–52. For a roundup of recent microeconomic work that finds relief programs stimulated consumption and reduced mortality but did not increase private employment, noting WPA jobs were often seen as more attractive than existing private sector jobs, see Price Fishback, "How Successful Was the New Deal? The Microeconomic Impact of New Deal Spending and Lending Policies in the 1930s," *Journal of Economic Literature* 55, no. 4 (December 2017): 1435–85.

93. Federal Writers' Project, *Florida: A Guide to the Southernmost State* (New York: Oxford University Press, 1956), xx, 3, 6.

94. See David J. Nelson, *How the New Deal Built Florida Tourism: The Civilian Conservation Corps and State Parks* (Gainesville: University Press of Florida, 2019).

95. Carita Doggett Corse to Henry Alsberg, May 23, 1939, enclosure, Zora Neale Hurston Corporate Subject File, Library of Congress, http://hdl.loc.gov/loc.afc/afcflwpa.essay1.

96. Federal Writers' Project, *Florida,* 3.

97. Christine Bold, *The WPA Guides: Mapping America* (Jackson: University Press of Mississippi, 1999), 189.

98. Victoria Grieve, *The Federal Art Project and the Creation of Middlebrow Culture* (Urbana: University of Illinois Press, 2010); Sharon Ann Musher, *Democratic Art: The New Deal's Influence on American Culture*

(Chicago: University of Chicago Press, 2015); also Amy Spellacy, "Mapping the Metaphor of the Good Neighbor: Geography, Globalism, and Pan-Americanism during the 1940s," *American Studies* 47, no. 2 (Summer 2006): 39–66.

CONCLUSION

1. Gabriel Debenedetti, "Biden Is Planning an FDR-Size Presidency," *New York Magazine,* May 11, 2020, https://nymag.com/intelligencer/2020/05/joe-biden-presidential-plans.html.

2. On government ownership and direction of wartime manufacturing, see Mark R. Wilson, *Destructive Creation: American Business and the Winning of World War II* (Philadelphia: University of Pennsylvania Press, 2016). For the federal budget, see *Historical Statistics of the United States, Earliest Times to the Present, Millennial Edition,* ed. Susan B. Carter et al., vol. 5, *Part E: Governance and International Relations,* (Cambridge: Cambridge University Press, 2006), 91–94, table Ea 636–43.

3. On the bailout and stimulus of 2008–9, see Eric Rauchway, "Neither a Great Depression nor a New Deal," in *The Presidency of Barack Obama: A First Historical Assessment,* ed. Julian E. Zelizer (Princeton: Princeton University Press, 2018), 30–44.

4. Franklin D. Roosevelt, "Address on Election of Liberals," November 4, 1938, in *The Public Papers and Addresses of Franklin D. Roosevelt,* vol. 7, *The Continuing Struggle for Liberalism* (New York: Macmillan, 1941), 584–93.

5. Franklin D. Roosevelt, "The Second Inaugural Address," January 20, 1937, in *The Public Papers and Addresses of Franklin D. Roosevelt,* vol. 6, *The Constitution Prevails* (New York: Macmillan, 1941), 1–6.

6. Franklin D. Roosevelt, "Annual Message to the Legislature," January 6, 1932, in *The Public Papers and Addresses of Franklin D. Roosevelt,* vol. 1, *The Genesis of the New Deal, 1928–1932* (New York: Random House, 1938), 111–26.

7. Franklin D. Roosevelt, "Annual Message to the Congress," January 3, 1934, *The Public Papers and Addresses of Franklin D. Roosevelt,* vol. 3, *The Advance of Recovery and Reform* (New York: Random House, 1938), 8–14.

8. Elizabeth Borgwardt, *A New Deal for the World: America's Vision for Human Rights* (Cambridge, MA: Belknap Press of Harvard University Press, 2005); also Scott J. Shapiro and Oona A. Hathaway, *The Internationalists: How a Radical Plan to Outlaw War Remade the World* (New York: Simon and Schuster, 2017).

9. Franklin D. Roosevelt, "Address at Ottawa, Canada," August 25, 1943, in *The Public Papers and Addresses of Franklin D. Roosevelt,* vol. 12, *The Tide Turns* (New York: Harper and Brothers, 1943), 365–69.

10. "The Atlantic Charter," August 14, 1941, in *The Public Papers and Addresses of Franklin D. Roosevelt,* vol. 10, *The Call to Battle* (New York: Harper and Brothers, 1941), 314–17.

11. United Nations Environment Programme, "Global Green New Deal Policy Brief," March 2009, https://wedocs.unep.org/bitstream/handle/20.500.11822/7903/A_Global_Green_New_Deal_Policy_Brief.pdf; "Recognizing the Duty of the Federal Government to Create a Green New Deal," House Resolution 109, February 7, 2019, https://www.congress.gov/bill/116th-congress/house-resolution/109?q=%7B%22search%22%3A%5B%22green+new+deal%22%5D%7D&s=1&r=5; "Recognizing the Duty of the Federal Government to Create a Green New Deal," Senate Resolution 59, February 7, 2019, https://www.congress.gov/bill/116th-congress/senate-resolution/59/text?q=%7B%22search%22%3A%5B%22green+new+deal%22%5D%7D&r=2&s=1.

acknowledgments

I am grateful to my friends and colleagues who have listened to and guided me, and especially those who have read and commented on the manuscript: Greg Downs, Ari Kelman, Kevin Kruse, Rachel St. John, and Louis Warren. At Yale University Press, Seth Ditchik knew I wanted to write something like this book, and I am glad he decided I should write it; thanks to him, Karen Olson, Margaret Otzel, and other staff at the press as well as the anonymous referees, and also to copyeditor Robin DuBlanc. As always, I owe most to my wife and fellow scholar of the New Deal, to whom this book is dedicated, and who not only read and commented on the manuscript but had to hear about it on more than one occasion: Kathy Olmsted.

index

African Americans, 103–32; anti-
lynching legislation and, 117–18,
128; election of 1932 and, 112–15;
election of 1936 and, 121; housing discrimination and, 118–20;
public works employment of,
63–65, 116, 124, 168, 205n85;
schools built for, 123–24; and
TVA, 63–64; voting by, 7, 107–9,
111, 114–15, 121, 128, 130–31. *See
also* racial discrimination
Agricultural Adjustment Act of
1933, 66, 91
Agricultural Adjustment Administration (AAA), 85, 87, 91, 94, 116
Agriculture Department, 68
airports, 5, 103–4, 135, 140, 155
Alabama Power Company, 48
Alcoa, Tennessee, 69
allotment policy, 77–79, 81, 83–84, 95
American Construction Council,
142–43

American Federation of Labor
(AFL), 110–11, 124, 156
American Guide Series, 171–73
American Indian Defense
Association, 82
Americans with Disabilities Act
of 1990, 139
American Youth Congress, 128
Anasazis, 76
anti-lynching legislation, 117–18,
128
Aquatic Park (San Francisco), 104,
168
Arlington National Cemetery,
13–14, 39
Army Corps of Engineers, 54
Arnautoff, Victor, 104–5
assimilation by Native Americans,
81, 97
Atlanta Daily World on 1932
election, 115
atomic weapons, 71–72

Golden Gate International Exposition (1939), 103
Goldschmidt, Arthur, 155, 156
gold standard, 153–54
Gompers, Samuel, 157
Gone with the Wind (film), 130–31
Grant, Ulysses S., 106
Grazing Service (Interior Department), 90, 91
"Green New Deal," 132, 178
Grubb, W. I., 66

Harding, Warren, 48, 79, 107
Hastie, William, 122, 129
Hearst, William Randolph, 30–31
Hitler, Adolf, 18–19, 33, 37
Home Owners Loan Corporation (HOLC), 105, 119
homesteading, 90
Hoover, Herbert: African Americans and, 107–10, 111; and Bonus Army, 16–27, 28–29; Depression and, 14–15; election campaign (1932), 149; and Muscle Shoals, 47, 48–49; Native Americans and, 81; on Tennessee Valley plan of Roosevelt, 52–53; unemployment and, 143–44; War Finance Corporation and, 201n40
Hoover Dam, 86
Hopis, 76
Hopkins, Harry: Civil Works Service and, 161; Committee on Economic Security and, 163–64; CWA and, 158–60, 162–63; Federal Art Project and, 140; FERA and, 153, 156–57; TERA

and, 146; WPA and, 124, 139–40, 166, 167, 176
hospitals, 86, 88, 98
housing discrimination, 105, 118–20, 132
Howard, Edgar, 95–96
Howe, Louis, 36–37, 83
Hunters Point (San Francisco), 103–4, 105, 132
Hurley, Patrick, 17, 23, 24, 34
Hurston, Zora Neale, 172, 173
Hushka, William, 13, 15, 21, 28
hydroelectric power, 46–47, 50–51, 61. *See also specific projects*

Ickes, Anna, 83
Ickes, Harold, 67, 83, 86, 90, 98, 123, 154–55
immigrants, 81, 141
Indian Citizenship Act of 1924, 79
Indian Emergency Conservation Work (IECW) program, 76, 85–87
Indian New Deal, 76, 84, 89, 99–100
Indian Oil Act of 1927, 79
Indian Reorganization Act (also known as the Wheeler-Howard Act), 6, 95–98
Indian Rights Association, 96
individualism, 77, 82, 83–84
industrial sector: American Construction Council and, 142–43; CWA and, 158; marginalized communities adversely impacted by, 105; National Defense Act and, 47; National Industrial

Shirley, Jim, 92
sidewalk construction projects, 5, 136–37, 140, 168, 174
Skidmore, Owings & Merrill, 71
smallpox, 80
Smith, Al, 108, 111, 115, 162
Smith, Ellison "Cotton Ed," 125
Smith v. Allwright (1943), 129–30
Social Security Act of 1935, 116, 138, 139, 164, 176
soil conservation, 85, 92
Spingarn, Joel, 112–13
Standard Oil, 78–79
Straus, Jesse, 146
Sunshine School (San Francisco), 104
Supreme Court (U.S.): Hoover's nominees for, 110; New Deal cases, 66, 67–68; on primary elections, 129–30; Roosevelt's nominees for, 127. *See also specific cases*

Taft, William Howard, 107
Taliman, Henry, 93
Tampa International Airport, 5
Taylor Grazing Act of 1934, 89–90
Teapot Dome scandal, 79
Temporary Emergency Relief Administration (TERA), 145–46, 152
tenant farmers, 56, 177
Tennessee Electric Power Company, 46
Tennessee Valley Authority (TVA): African Americans employed by, 63–65; African American workers and, 116; dam construction by, 55;

electricity generation by, 6, 43–44; job creation by, 59; mission of, 53; privatization of utilities and, 47–49, 53; soil conservation policies, 85. *See also* Norris Dam
Tomb of the Unknowns, 13
Treasure Island (San Francisco), 103
Treasury Department, 20
tuberculosis, 80
Tugwell, Rexford, 33, 38, 65, 66, 152
Tydings, Millard, 125

unemployment: COVID-19 pandemic's impact on, 175; Depression's impact on, 164; global financial crisis (2008) and, 177; Hoover's policies and, 15; private sector's failure to remedy, 110; public works projects and, 139, 143–45; Roosevelt (Theodore) and, 82
unemployment insurance, 6, 28, 32–34, 138, 151–52, 164, 176
unions. *See* labor unions
United Nations Environment Programme, 178
United States v. Classic (1941), 129–30
University of California, Davis, 4
Urban League, 122

Vann, Robert, 108, 111
veterans, 24. *See also* Bonus Expeditionary Force
Veterans Administration, 159–60
voting rights, 79, 106, 109, 111, 128–30

Eric Rauchway is distinguished professor of history at the University of California, Davis, and is the author of several books, most recently *Winter War: Hoover, Roosevelt, and the First Clash Over the New Deal, The Money Makers: How Roosevelt and Keynes Ended the Depression, Defeated Fascism, and Secured a Prosperous Peace,* and *The Great Depression and the New Deal: A Very Short Introduction.*

Featuring intriguing pairings of authors and subjects, each volume in the Why X Matters series presents a concise argument for the continuing relevance of an important idea.

Also in the series